Frontispiece

Eva Zeisel:
A Soviet Prison Memoir

Recounting 16 months in a Soviet prison, 1936 – 37
Compiled and Edited by
Jean Richards & Brent C. Brolin
with essays by
Jean Richards
Karen Kettering, Ph.D. and
Edward P. Gazur, Special Agent F.B.I.

Notice of Rights

Acknowledgments

Thanks...

To Andras Koerner, who started the ball rolling by showing this memoir to Istvan Deak, who passed it on to Edwin Frank, who tossed it to Brigid Hughes, who published a portion of it in her magazine, *A Public Space*.

To our friend, Karen Kettering, the most efficient, thorough, and knowledgeable historian of Russian art we know, and to her Russian archival guru, Svetlana Chestnykh, who helped decipher handwriting and provide background information. All Russian documents are courtesy of Karen, as are her translations.

To the late Ed and Ruth Gazur, whose amazing discoveries gave us goosebumps, and with whom we formed a close bond.

To our charming cousin, Jean Radvanyi, former Director of the French Research Center, Moscow, who enthusiastically dug for and found additional documents in that city.

To our beloved cousin, John Striker, for his foresight in insisting that we record these memories back in the 1970s.

To our old friend, Bob Halasz, for repeated proofreading and copyediting.

Mainly to Brent C. Brolin, who spent months putting this eBook together, even as the technology was developing beneath his fingers.

And to Eva, my adventurous mother, from whom we have all learned so much about how to live.

Jean Richards

Eva Zeisel:
A Soviet Prison Memoir

Arrest in Moscow

Memories of long ago are not true. They have been gilded by time. The happenings I write down, the way I remember them now, with love for my youth, sentimentally, memories of times long past, of myself—slim, young and energetic, strong, resistant, sad and alert. I speak of myself as much as of the things that happened to me. None of it is true, but I shall be precise reporting my memories.

It all started with mother bending over me to wake me up. It all ended with this. This, for a long time was the end of my good life. Even today, this one moment, to which I could not think back, to the warmth flooding my heart, and my heart repudiating this memory energetically and with bitterness, even now, I think of this moment when Mother bent over me to wake me up as one of the happiest of my life. I smiled up at her. I had slept particularly well, probably dreamt very happily and when I saw her bend over me, I put my arms around her neck and we smiled at each other. Only four o'clock in the morning, hardly light, and no time to get up.

The day before, I had walked home through the park from the administration offices of the State China and Glass Trust where I worked. I had been particularly cheerful and I had smiled, stopped on the way. I do not remember why it was such a happy day. After work, I had gone to the beauty parlor and had my nails manicured, my hair done, and a facial massage. I felt pretty when I got back to the office to have a meeting with—funny, I've forgotten his name. He was the higher boss of the office. I remember now. His name was Gottwald. Between him and me there was a flirting atmosphere. He was a good-looking, broad-shouldered, friendly man. Our flirtation had proceeded just a bit further. I had to walk through the park to come home, and it was May 25, 1936. There were many people in the open library of the park, lying there after work, in reclining chairs, children playing. Everything seemed clean and friendly. I do not remember the evening. Mother and I shared a room in the little apartment in Moscow we rented with my brother, his wife and small child. After dinner together, we must have had a good evening before I went to bed.

And now Mother was bending over me to wake me up. Mother was very pretty, but it was not customary between us that she was openly tender or loving. So, when she bent over me, her smile and her understanding, maybe her kiss (this I forget), must have come as an unexpected present after a good day and a good night, after a life where everything seemed to go so well, full of spring, of clean, fragrant flowering bushes on the way home from work, and children playing.

"Well," Mother said, "There are some people here to see you." I looked around and saw a woman and, I think, the building supervisor.

"What do they want?"

"Oh, they want to talk to you."

But when I found out they wanted to search the apartment, I was upset. It never occurred to me that I could have done something wrong. Maybe some misunderstanding. Not even then did it occur to me that something might happen to me personally.

I got up and put on my housecoat, a green checkered one of wool flannel. I do not even recall what they wanted to see. Suddenly there were more men in the room. They looked at my letters and at my photographs. I think by that time I became quite ill at ease, maybe a little scared. They went through my photographs and stopped at two of them. One was an enlarged snapshot of me on a beach with my eyes closed. It looked like a mask, a mask of my dead face, and the men passed the photograph from one to the other and they smiled, and it scared me. Later on, it scared me more. I do not know whether I realized then or later that they thought I would soon be dead.

They also found a picture of a gun, an enlargement I had made when I bought my beautiful camera, seven years earlier. It had been the fashion at that time to make partial enlargements of things so they looked like something else. Like speaking a word over and over again and changing the meaning of a syllable. At the time I got my camera, which I had bought from my first earnings, I took pictures of dolls' heads because I lived with a family, near the German factory where I worked, that had a little girl. I took pictures of her dolls' heads, heads of broken dolls and I also took a picture of her father's pistol, a tiny gun, with many little bullets laid out in a row, and I enlarged it into a pattern. Now they took that photograph and passed it around. They took other photographs too, and they also looked at them with interest. It must have been interesting for them to see what a foreigner had among her letters and photographs and personal belongings.

I really do not remember where they looked and for what. But I do remember feeling life receding from me and myself being set apart. They were not rude. They were extremely polite.

After a while they said, "Well, you'd better come along." This was a shock. I had not thought of this up to that moment. They showed me a paper, the order for my arrest.[1] They had shown me the upper part of this paper when they came in, and now they showed me the whole thing; it said, "The Arrest of Eva Alexandrovna Stricker." The woman told me to get dressed and pack my things. I started to pack a few clothes and Mother helped. Then the woman said, "Take more handkerchiefs, you might need them." And I wondered, and said, "Just for a few days? It can't be for long." The woman answered, "Just take your handkerchiefs and a little more underwear." She watched while I dressed.

My garter was broken. The button that held the stocking was missing. As usual in such cases, when I didn't have a penny or a *kopeck* I took a little piece of paper, folded it into a square and put it into my garter-holder to hold my stocking. The woman pointed towards the wad of paper and said, "Give me that piece of paper." She unfolded the little piece of newspaper, which was not much bigger than a fifty-cent piece, noted that this had been clandestinely put into my stocking, and took it away. I asked her whether I could talk to my mother alone and she said no, only in front of her. I started to say, "Please call this man. There must be a misunderstanding," but the woman would not let me continue.

I had to go through the other room, where my brother and his family lived. When I passed them, my brother Michael had a doll is his hand, a puppet, and holding the arm of the puppet between his fingers, he waved its little hand to me: "good-bye." And even now when I think of it, I must cry. The baby was in the corner sleeping. Michael smiled at me and waved the little hand of the puppet. And my heart broke because it had become soft. I do not know whether I kissed my mother good-bye. I might have, under the eyes of this woman.

Then we all walked down to the car. The light of the morning had flooded the courtyard, unexpectedly grey and cold. It was a new day,

---

[1] No "arrest" document was found in the file. The closest thing was the "accusation and decision to imprison" Eva, dated June 2, 1936.

and my heart was not sinking anymore. I was so sure to be back in a few days.

As we came down, the man and woman asked the building supervisor to cut them some branches from the flowering bushes surrounding the house, and he got a knife and cut them big branches of flowers, Japanese cherries and peach blossoms. They took the branches in their arms and filled the open car with flowers. I sat in the back, between two of them. There were two more plus the driver, and the car was filled with flowers. When this happened, it seemed to me so incongruous that I forgot that it was me they had arrested, and I smiled. "Here am I arrested among so many flowers," I thought, "It's spring, and they are taking me among the flowers."

One of them turned back and asked the other, "Do you have a cigarette?" I had some, and offered my packet to him saying, "Here, have one." But he refused. He was quite strict, almost shocked at the thought of taking a cigarette from me. Suddenly I understood that I was not any more a part of the people who were well, healthy and harmless. To take a cigarette from me was wrong. I was rebuked, I was set apart, and my heart fell again. They asked, "Where else do you have any of your things?" I told them I had been given an apartment recently. I had not yet moved into it, but had some things there.

"What sort of things?"

"Old newspapers," I said.

I had to put something in there, to take possession, kind of like a squatter, so I had some old suitcases filled with newspapers.

We went to my new apartment. It was a large, empty room. I was to have half of it, but the partitions were not up yet. They said, "Eva Alexandrovna, is this all you have?" And with their saying "Eva Alexandrovna," I felt a part of humanity again. It was good to be called by my name and my father's name, and for this I was grateful to them. They asked me where else I had things. I told them there were a few more things at a friend's where I had slept in the maid's room for a while before moving in with my brother a short time ago. But we did not go there. They took me instead to the Butyrka, the famous, terrible prison, the Butyrka, which I had often passed these last few weeks thinking of this or that person who had disappeared there.

But now I do not remember entering the Butyrka. I do not remember the door opening and closing behind me. I don't remember the questions they asked me. I do remember one courtyard after the other, and I remember the small room that was my cell. I remember walking through the courtyards with a Red soldier behind me, being led to be searched, showered and photographed.

I was surprised that the photographer was just a simple man, like any photographer, who asked me to look forward and sideways. He put a number in front of my chest and I thought, "This will make me look like those pictures of criminals one sees, 'Wanted for Murder.'" Then they took me to be fingerprinted, one finger rolled in the ink after the other, and again I thought, It's like the movies.

Again, we walked through many courtyards and the funny thing was that I did not see anybody. It was all empty. Whether this was because people were sleeping, as it was still very early, or for some other reason I do not know, but it was empty. Finally, I was in my cell, and I still did not know what it was all about.

My heart was not really heavy, not appropriately heavy, not as heavy as it should be or not as heavy as you might think it was, or ought to have been. The cell was really a small room with a wooden floor. The wooden floor made it look more like a room. And it was not square; it was part of a round building so it was lopsided and had an irregular window with a shield in front of it so you could not see out. But of course, there were bars in front of the window. This was to be expected, after all, it was a prison. In the corner stood a bucket, and that was terrible. It smelled and it was an indignity. There were two cots in the room, like beds. At the time, I did not know that they would later have to be attached to the walls, but the fact that there were cots, and that it was a room, seemed to make it less terrifying.

I sat down and looked around. It had been a long day, a long morning. Much had happened, much had changed. Here was a new life and I had to be in control of it. I knew that every thought from now on was to be the work of my mind. I thought of the car trip. The trip had been beautiful. We had driven through town, through the waking city and past the house of my last lover. His curtains were drawn. He lived just on the second floor, and I had looked up and smiled and thought, "Here I pass your house." We had driven in the open car, full of flowers, past my lover who was asleep, to the prison. I smiled, it was funny. Later I wrote a poem about it.

Natasha

But now here I was in prison. Every so often something would strike me as funny, like the pussycat outside the cell. It was Natasha's pussycat. Natasha was my cellmate. I do not think that Natasha was in bed when I came, so it must have been morning by the time I reached the cell. No one was rude. The guard outside our cell was quite kind. Not that he spoke to us, but he was inoffensive, and that was good. And there was Natasha, the softest, dirtiest, warmest, friendliest girl. Natasha, the most Russian girl. I do not know what had happened to her. She had been arrested just the day before I arrived; taken from a train on the way to visit her aunt with a basket full of food and a pussycat. The pussycat outside the cell was calling and Natasha said, "My pussycat is meowing." And it made my heart sad, and inside my heart cried because with her pussycat meowing it was hard for me to exclude all the soft thoughts of love and life and warmth. But the pussycat kept meowing, and reminding me of how small and helpless a pussycat can be, and how life can be the same way. In prison it is much easier to think of abstract things, bracing oneself; but when a pussycat breaks through your armor, it is hard to defend yourself from unplanned thoughts.

We spent the day together. Natasha sat on her cot and told me she had once been in a theater. It had been so beautiful. They had played Eugene Onegin and she knew it by heart. She sat there for a long time, maybe all day, and in a singsong voice recited the poem to me. I do not know who Natasha was but she certainly was the most neglected thing I ever saw. The sweetest, the kindest, and the poorest. She was very young. There was something fuzzy about her, and her underwear was so dirty.

I had been there three days. Natasha had already been called out to her investigator and, from time to time, she said she ought to think about her affairs. She still had some food from the provisions she was taking to her aunt, and she shared it with me. She also had a cake of cheap, perfumed, pink soap. The wonderful smell—nice, strong, cheap smell of soap—mixed with the smell of the bucket. It did not bother her so much, so she washed the bucket for both of us.

By the third day, my heart had fallen low. Nothing had happened, nobody had asked for me; I seemed to be forgotten, entirely forgotten. I had to build up patience so I searched my memory. I remembered two stories. One of my friends had been in prison. He had never been the same again. People had been taken out of his cell to be shot. People he had shared his days with were taken to be shot one after another. His turn never came; he was reprieved, but he was never the same again. It had been very heavy to bear, he told me.

And I thought of Natasha Bam's husband, who had been in prison for just six months, the usual time for an investigation. After his release he was unable to work; he turned away from life, turned away from his wife and baby. He now lived alone, without hope, without work, a sick man. He had been a well-known art critic and art historian, a brilliant person.

Knowing all this, I decided I had to amuse myself if I was to live. I had to entertain myself. I had to find the thoughts that would keep me alive. I had to do gymnastics; I had to live a controlled life which must start immediately. It did not take long to understand that my life in prison was going to be a constant surprise, that no part of my life would be within my control except my sanity, that all I could do was to keep sane.

On the third day they took me away. Quite unexpectedly, I heard my name through the little peephole in the door. They usually called you by asking, "What is your name?" (They do this so that others cannot hear your name, because it might not be your real name, or, because if it is, it might be revealed to others.) The shutter is opened with a metallic rattle. A man looks into the peephole and says, "What is your name?" Then, "Dress! Put on your things for the investigation!" And that might mean hope; that might mean going home.

Now the voice said, "Bring your things with you." So I packed my belongings into a scarf (or perhaps it was a kerchief or a paper bag), said good-bye to Natasha, and walked through the courtyards again; two men in front and two in back of me.

I entered the prison van from the back. To the left and the right were small cubbyholes, and I was put into one of them. There were no windows. You knew you were driving through town, but you did not know where you were going. I had the feeling that Hermann Fuhlbrügge, my German modelmaker, was in one of the other cubbyholes. This again struck me as funny. I do not know why it struck me as funny, because it was really rather sordid.[2] [2]

---

[2] "Transportation of prisoners about the city was in vehicles which resembled delivery vans and were often labeled 'Bread' or 'meat," to make them seem harmless to

It was undignified to be driven around Moscow in a cubbyhole, but it was an experience which did not happen to everyone. Whether I was pleased, I do not know, but I certainly was not happy.

The next thing I remember was that we were standing among thousands of people in a huge hall or railroad station with a glass dome over it, and I had to go with a woman to undress me to see whether I had something on me which did not belong there. I was most surprised because all these people were waiting for something, waiting to go somewhere. They were all prisoners. It was nighttime. It was not gruesome, although it made a Gogolesque impression, or a scene from Hogarth or Daumier.

A young girl in uniform took charge of me and the next thing I remember was that we boarded a train. It was a regular passenger train, with one car reserved for prisoners. I remember the sound of our steps as we walked into this car, the young girl and I. I walked past cages that had been compartments. In one of the first cages sat my modelmaker, Fuhlbrügge, head in hands, with flaming red hair and stubble, unkempt, apparently exploding with fury and indignation. This kindly, clean-cut, neat, harmless petit bourgeois, who was always spotless, now looked like the image of a hardened criminal. It made me laugh aloud. Here, I thought, was great cause for mirth. He did not notice me as we walked by.

And here was my cage, further down in the same car. The girl locked the door behind me. In the corridor was a commander, a kindly sort of person, quite good-looking, loud-voiced, friendly. He admonished the criminals in the next cage—there were a lot of them, loud, dirty-mouthed, vulgar—to mind their language because of the lady next door.

I had my own attendant accompanying me. A quiet, uncommunicative, unsmiling, young girl in a uniform. She was stationed just outside my cage. All the windows were painted over. You could not see the station or the people waving good-bye, or the landscape as it passed.

We were going to Leningrad, away from anybody who cared. I was getting deeper into it. My feelings embraced me now and pulled me

---

the population. Inside they were divided into several compartments, ventilated by tiny holes, in which a man had barely enough room to stand or sit." F. Beck and W. Godin, *Russian Purge and the Extraction of Confession*, trans. Eric Mosbacher and David Porter (New York: The Viking Press, 1951) p. 63.

in—away from what had been my life. I was puzzled, but a dullness had settled on me. I was traveling. There were long wooden benches—two on each side. My "luggage" was taken from me. I heard the life on the platform, the rebellious shouts of the prisoners next door, and for the first time I was alone, alone with nothing in the world.

I sat facing front. There was nothing to look at. In my hand I held two clean sanitary napkins. They smelled of disinfectant. All trains in Russia smell like poor people, like clothes worn for years. All trains where poor people have sat and slept are impregnated with this smell forever. And this train did not smell different.

The trip to Leningrad took very long. I was alone with the thoughts I had to produce in order to keep my heart from sinking. I hoped I would have to pass Fuhlbrügge's cage on my way to the bathroom, but we only passed the cage jammed full of criminals. The girl waited outside the bathroom door. It was smelly; no water came from the faucet.

At one of the stations there was a loud commotion, crying and shouting. Prisoners were being loaded. When it became too rough in the next cage, the commander again cheerfully admonished the criminals to stop the obscenities because of me. I smiled. I was still part of the outside world.

At mealtime, I got a can of baked beans. They were cold and heavy. I think I also got some boiling water, *kipiatok*; it fills the body and makes the blood circulate. The male prisoners next door got stinking herring. I could not have eaten it, I thought. I could hardly eat my beans because of the smell of the herring. But they fought for it.

We arrived in Leningrad after a long night on a hard bench. I had slept with my cheek touching the two sanitary napkins which were like clean little pillows covered with gauze. I saw Fuhlbrügge get out first, reluctantly and rebelliously; he was pushed into the van. I got out after him and was put into a black limousine.

I had not washed that morning, but unsmilingly, in the smelly toilet of the train, my attendant had offered me her lipstick, comb, and pocket mirror. As we got into the limousine she sat to my left. There were also several armed guards, and we drove through Leningrad. I remember seeing the heavy gates of my new prison swing open. At that moment the girl turned her head and looked at me. She was so scared and so full of pity and awe that it gripped my heart; was she wondering what I felt, thinking I would never come out of there? I never saw her after that.

Bolshoi Dom: Leningrad

The Cupboard

I was taken to an office, searched again, and then taken through many corridors. I was put into a cupboard.[3][3] My bundle had been returned to me; it meant this was the place I was going to stay, I thought. The cupboard was not light, but it was not dark either, because you are never left in the dark. Light came in above the door.

When I had been with Natasha, close to home, close to Mother, I was not really on my own. I was not really alone. But here in Leningrad, where I had not been for two years, I was entirely among strangers. I had no friends, I had no business here. I felt abandoned. This must be a gigantic misunderstanding, and it would take time to sort it out. I did not doubt that I would get out. But meanwhile, I had better adjust to the situation.

The difference between my life now and my life just three or four days before was so great and so baffling that I somehow accepted the fact that I was now in a cupboard. From the grunts and snorts I heard, my modelmaker, Fuhlbrügge, must have been in a nearby cell or cupboard. He sounded like a rhinoceros.

This was my first chance to prove to myself that I was impervious to inconveniences such as living in a cupboard, and I decided to make myself as comfortable as possible and to keep up my spirits as well as I could. So now I was in complete charge of the cupboard. I sat up on the bench, sideways, and tried to straighten my legs. This was not possible. The cupboard was not wide enough. That was not good, as it is necessary sometimes to straighten one's legs. And then I tried other positions. I tried to lie down on my back with my knees pulled up, embryo-style, but this, too, was not very comfortable, even though I used my little bundle of belongings as a pillow. It was not as bad as all

---

[3] "In some jails prisoners waiting for interrogation, or waiting before or after removal to another prison, were put into what were called 'kennels.' These were tiny compartments in which prisoners were often kept for hours, or even for half a day at a time. Abandonment in such cubbyholes, apparently inadvertent, was one of the 'cultural' methods of softening up." F. Beck and W. Godin, *Russian Purge…*, trans. Eric Mosbacher and David Porter (New York: The Viking Press, 1951), p. 63.

that, but it was not really good. Well, I thought, if I can't bend my legs, if I can't keep my legs straight, if I can't get my knees comfortable curling up on the bench, either sideways or lying on my back, I'll be rather cramped in this cupboard. I thought the first thing is to get good brisk movement and circulation because good spirits are dependent on it. And with the vigor of my convictions, I started to do gymnastics, first waving my arms as far as possible, one at a time. I tried to stand on my shoulder, then on my head. This was rather easy and comfortable in the cupboard, because there is not too much room to fall. You can support yourself by touching the walls. Here I was in the cupboard, standing on my head, my skirt falling down over my face, when I noticed that the little round peephole did not close as fast as before, and I burst out laughing, thinking of the guard at the other end and his puzzled, surprised face. Then I turned right side up again and sat down. My work well done, the gloom conquered and rejected, I started to plan my days.

Since everything up to now had been so surprising and illogical, I expected that this cupboard was the place I would have to adjust to for some time. I thought it would be quite easy to go insane in this situation, so the work ahead needed energy and planning. I was prepared to sort my thoughts into good, long ones—those that were permitted—and those that were to be forbidden. Every so often, I had to stop my mind from wandering. Every so often, the picture of my mother crept into my mind or passed on the horizon, her bending over me, her smile, her prettiness, her warmth, her last moment with me. These thoughts I had to brutally put away. This, the most dangerous thought, forced a spasm in my chest that forced the tears up into my eyes, poured a flush of warmth over my face and my shoulders, and a longing—deep, strong, and painful—for life just out of my reach; for life now, for love, and for the days I had left behind.

This was the taboo of my days. I knew, if I were going to allow myself to think of the sun outside, of mother, of my work, of the flirt in the office, of my lover waiting—the big, lovely good-looking boy—that my sanity would not be safe. That I, too, would bang the walls and throw myself around like Fuhlbrügge, who was rebelling in the cupboard next to mine. I, too, was close to becoming an animal. Righteousness was not here to guide me in the cupboard. I understood that it was I who was now my whole world. In me was all the power for beauty and dignity and strength, and I sat down on my bench and started to think a beautiful thought. A thought of far away and long ago.

My Cell

I do not know how long I was in the cupboard, how I got out of it, or who took me. But soon I was alone in a cell. I pushed away the feeling of finality, but I was frightened. Natasha, the train ride, even the cupboard had held suspense. Now I was scared that I would be forgotten. The big metallic door fell into place and the big key was retrieved. I listened. I was alone. No one, nothing was there to tie me to my life except a small bundle of my things. Mother does not know where I am. She'll be looking for me. She has not the slightest idea that I am here. I sat down on the bed, on the mattress, then I got up and stood facing the window. It was gloomy. No sun reached this cell. I looked around. The last sound had been the turning of the large key locking me in. Not even a sound of the retreating steps.

The heavy wall facing the door slanted back at an angle toward the small, high, recessed window which opened by tilting inwards. A metal shield in front of the window blocked the view. To the right of it, in a corner, was the toilet. Above the toilet, a water box with a metallic handle and chain. I noticed that the chain was attached to the handle with a wire, and I wondered: a removable object? The wire? Then the sink and faucet. There was a crack around the faucet. On the wall under the sink was a grille. It was not for heat. I do not know what it was, but much later squeaks of baby rats came from this grille. Then, jutting out of the wall, a small, metal folding table. Next came a pipe from ceiling to floor, a folding shelf to sit on and two metal shelves high on the wall for clothes. Facing the window, the door. No handle; a round peephole with a square wicket under it that also locked, and which gave a rhythmic tuck-a-tuck-a-tuck noise when it was opened. Above the door was another little grille that could accommodate a listening device; to hear my thoughts, I supposed. Then a piece of wall and another corner. Facing the little, attached stool was the bed without legs, that folded up against the wall. On it a mattress and blanket. At the end of the bed was an empty space long enough for another bed. Then came the other corner and the wall with the window. The floor was grey cement and the walls were painted dull green. When I stepped back toward the door I could see a small stretch of sky and a roof with one row of windows, and when I craned my neck I could see a fire escape running along the top floor. The cell was six and one-half paces, walking diagonally. ("Marching Rhyme," which I wrote later, was composed with the same meter: six and one-half paces to the end of each line.)

I sat down on the mattress. Time passed. I folded my clothes carefully on the two small shelves. My hand lingered on one blouse. It was of white silk with embroidered flower buds to the left and to the right of a jabot of little pleats. I was wearing a good skirt and a waist-length jacket. There was a narrow-waisted dress of brown wool, also embroidered with small flowers. It had always disturbed me that the hem was not quite even. I also had my green and black checkered woolen housecoat, which I had made. It had a wide, pointed collar with hand-crocheted black woolen lace. And then there were the handkerchiefs, some underwear, a toothbrush, and ankle-high, red Saffian slippers with soft sheep's wool inside and a glamorous, cheerful, long, shaggy fairy-tale beard all around the top. I put them down and feasted my eyes on them.

Then I found Natasha's fragrant, pink, lovely soap, which I had taken by mistake. I felt terribly sorry for having taken her most treasured possession, and I thought of her. I smelled it for a long time. It was luxurious. The cheap, pink soap was now my great treasure. I put it on the sink.

I cannot explain the quality of time, but time had to be conquered. Time had to be dealt with, filled. Time had to be gnawed at and time was gnawing at me. Time is your project, your problem. Time is the emptiness and fullness of cell No. 4.

After a little while, I understood that although I was perfectly alone, very close to me there was another person, equally perfectly alone. I did not know as yet the topography of my cellblock. But I knew that to the left and right were other people. Who? My heart was heavy. I felt abandoned. (There was still a certain novelty in the little wicket door opening and in each word spoken. There were very few words in the cell block.) Then I lay down without sheets. I think I had a towel, which I put against my face, turning toward the wall. The wicket opened and a voice said, "We must see your face." I think there was a compromise about a stocking covering my eyes and then I fell asleep into uncontrolled happiness and sweetness and love and beauty and color. I woke up with a thud.

The first day no sun ray entered. There was nothing by which to count the minutes or hours or to fill them, because you have to have a measure of time to be able to plan time and to fill it. I had no idea why I was there. But, in those first few days, my life changed. I revolted against the injustice of being kept a prisoner. I had to take hold of myself. I combed my hair. I walked to the toilet, looked into the distorted mirror of the toilet bowl, and wondered. I looked at my nails. They were still pink and clean and the polish was still intact. Later, when the polish began to fade, I wrote this poem.

We were not allowed to lie down until evening, although the first day I did lie down. Around the middle of the morning of the second day, a lovely thing happened. A ray of sun came into the cell and stayed there for about an hour. I watched it move slowly over the floor. And every day when the weather was fine it came at a certain time and made a sharp break on the wall, between a strongly lit patch on the surface of the dull green wall and the darkness at its edge, and moved slowly, until there was just a little spot before it left the cell.

Markings on the wall

The first time the sun ray entered my cell and passed over the tilted wall below the window I noticed groups of little lines scratched into the paint. Four straight lines, crosshatched with a fifth. There were many of these groups. Those who had been here before me had scratched a line each day, and there were two rows of scratches. When five days and nights had been consumed, minute by minute, they crossed the lines. It gripped my heart because I could not imagine anybody being that long in this cell. I still expected that any moment the door would open, the misunderstanding would be cleared up, and I would be permitted to return to the good life through an open gate.

As the sun ray continued through my cell, reaching the wall above the little table, I saw the name "Anni Helme" scratched into the wall along with two dates. She had had time to scratch in the date of her departure. It was not long ago, and between the two dates was six months. Six months! It was inconceivable! I despaired completely. It was terrifying. Annie Helme—where had she gone? What had happened to her? Where was she now? The cell held no more information. I wanted to break the chain of prisoners through this cell.

My thoughts started to form a broad, confused delta flowing and intertwining, getting muddled, leading to a sea of desperation. From time to time, my eyes went up to the loop of wire connecting the lever of the water box to the chain of the toilet. This copper wire that could be removed held some hope for freedom of action. But something had to be done about my thoughts. They had to be disentangled and kept straight. Something had to be done about time! The mass of time had to be cut up into sections, measured, dealt with. The only regular measures were the meals, and the gay measure of the ray of the sun between its point of entrance and its point of departure. Time had to be filled, and the days kept in order. However few days there were to be in this cell, they would have to be kept in order. I had to keep track of them without carving a third group of little lines into the wall. It is easy to forget their number and it adds to the confusion in the mind not to know the number of days. There is nothing to go by if one loses count.

Without any sign on my face, the tears flowed within me. My heart dropped. Fright gripped me. I reacted physically. My heart had to be kept under control. My temper, impatience, my feeling of injustice, my sense of urgency, my revolt against what happened to me—all had to be subdued—serenity, a dignified behavior had to be established and kept up.

Noises

I have not spoken about the noises of the night. Sometimes it seemed as if people were crying, but it was the doves in the early morning— cooing and making love. For a long time I thought it was the prisoners. I had the feeling that somewhere people were moaning at night; of course, it was the pigeons who were cooing. But pigeons sound as if they are moaning. You fill, with your imagination, this whole terrible atmosphere. You fill it with fear and suspicion about what is happening to other people.

I had the feeling there was a tremendous amount of noise, even though it was tremendously quiet. You could not even hear when somebody came to open the peephole on your cell door. In front of each cell was a rubber mat, and the guards wore felt slippers, so you hardly ever heard anybody walk, except a prisoner walking up the metal steps to the doctor, or a door opening or shutting with a bang, or the big soup bucket when it came around, or when a key turned somewhere in the four stories. Every noise was metallic; there was no noise that was not metallic. The soup bucket was metallic, the going up the steps was metallic, the turning of the key was metallic.

In the emptiness of the cell, the slightest and quietest noise became mountain-high, gruesome, disturbing. There is a mystery about noise. It contains all the ghosts of all the terrible things you ever heard of, cruelty behind each small noise. Each noise was so weighty that when I later told an investigator I could not sleep because there was so much noise, he said "Noise? In the prison cell? It's absolutely quiet!"

Exercises

One of the first memories, even before I was called out for the first time, was being taken out to walk in the courtyard. I was not alone, there was another girl, and it was sunny. After all, it was the end of May, beginning of June. The girl was limping. We walked around as the guard watched. We did not walk side by side; she was 180 degrees from me. And as she walked, she was smiling up at the sun. Our walk lasted seven minutes. She walked into the prison ahead of me and as she walked the last few steps she skipped in her limping way, looking up at the sun, smiling and skipping. That was an unforgettable image. I never saw her again.

Interrogation Begins

Nikultsev

I do not know exactly at which point I was first called out, but I was stewing in this Leningrad cell for about two weeks—for a long time I did not know which prison. About three weeks had passed altogether, but it seemed endlessly long.

The first time I was called out, I was taken to a large, elegant office and there was Mr. Nikultsev, who spoke with me in German. He was a very quiet, nice person. He was in no way slimy or playing games. I think he started to ask me who my friends were. I saw him each day for about a week, late in the evenings. At around midnight, he would have tea brought in, and usually a cheese sandwich and caviar. He had not yet told me why I was there. I did not yet understand. I think pretty soon I did. But I still believed, all through the time I saw him, that once this misunderstanding was cleared up I would be let go. I certainly did not think my life was in danger. Soon thereafter I was seen by him and a Commissar Berman together. (I did not know at the time who Berman was, but I found out later that Boris Berman was second-in-command of the NKVD. Much later I read that Berman was in charge of investigating and "arranging" the international relationships and friendships of the great accused, such as Radek and Bukharin, in preparation for the first Moscow show trials. Of course, I did not know that then.) Berman asked me for the names of people I knew in foreign lands, and I mentioned Arthur Koestler and Anna Seghers, who was a good Communist. I found out later that the NKVD did question both Koestler and Anna Seghers about me. I did not mention my aunt, Ilona [Duczynska] Polanyi, because I knew she was always too far on the left or too far on the right. (Much later I found out that she was a friend of Berman's. She had known him when she lived in Moscow right after the 1919 Hungarian Revolution.) Now Berman sat at the desk and Nikultsev sat next to him.

On my way to this meeting I had seen Bykhovskii, a former colleague, in the corridor. He had looked at me in a cockeyed sort of way—kind of pale and apologetic. I have to tell you about Bykhovskii. He was a Latvian Jew. He had worked as a technical engineer at the Lomonosov porcelain factory in Leningrad while I was there. Although Bykhovskii had never been unpleasant to me, and surely liked me, I found him to be a disagreeable, slimy sort of person. He was married, his wife was in Moscow, and he had a brother who was a doctor. His wife had worked in the German Trade Commission in Berlin with my mother's cousin, Ernö Seidler. About two weeks before I was arrested, I had met this cousin at a party. He had been a Hungarian revolutionary, a leader of the Red Army defending Budapest against the Romanians who marched in bringing Fascism. Today there is a big plaque on one of the streets in Hungary saying he defended Budapest, and my mother always said, "That's why we lost it!" Seidler was a very gentle, gentle, lovely person and a good friend of mine in Russia. (He was later shot.)

At this party Seidler told me Bykhovskii's wife had said that, had Bykhovskii not already been married, he would have married me. This was told to me but it did not impress me very much.

Bykhovskii had been arrested before me, and now I passed him in the corridor, on my way to see Berman. I smiled at him and he turned away. I did not know it yet, but Bykhovskii was my accuser.[4] Berman spoke quite nicely to me and then showed me a piece of paper that was the accusation. I remember that as he handed it to me he said, "Bykhovskii accuses you of wanting to kill Stalin."

This was Bykhovskii's accusation. That he had met me, that I had been very hostile to Stalin in my conversations, that he had tried to hold me back in my hostility, but that it had not worked. That I had said Stalin ought to be killed and I knew somebody who was an excellent shot, namely my modelmaker, Fuhlbrügge, whom I had invited to Russia to work with me, but who was really to be my triggerman. I do not know exactly what else was written there, but this was the worst possible accusation: to have plotted a terrorist act, an *attentat* [assassination attempt] on the Great Leader. It was not just that I knew about it. It was that I had insisted that I wanted to kill the leader.

Of course, I thought I would be shot. I think I started to cry. My tears were coming, my nose was running. I remember I had a blue jacket on,

---

[4] "Everyone was required to denounce at least one other person who had 'recruited' him—i.e., had persuaded him to engage in counter-revolutionary activity and had directed him. Everyone was also required to denounce as many other people as possible whom he had himself recruited." p. 45, F. Beck and W. Godin, Russian Purge..., trans. Eric Mosbacher and David Porter, (New York: The Viking Press, 1951).

and I wiped my nose with the back of my hand, my tears and my nose. Berman said, "Look what you're doing, look what you're doing, you make your hand dirty." And I said, "Well, that's the least of my troubles, and you wouldn't worry about that if you had gotten what I have just been given here."

"Oh yes," he said, "I have been in prison."

"But there must have been a reason," I answered. "After all, you must have fought for the Revolution."

"Oh, no, I was in prison under this regime."

"Well, certainly not with this sort of paper!" I replied, and he kind of laughed.

It was comforting to think that he had survived and was sitting behind his desk. I am quite sure that he was telling the truth.

Then he asked me when I had seen Bykhovskii last, and I told him, "Just now, outside in the corridor." He and Nikultsev looked at each other. Then I asked "Should I not have said that? Was that a [a mistake in the stage direction]?" And one of them answered, "We don't make mistakes in staging."

At that time, and even years later, I felt that Nikultsev had come to find out whether the accusation was true, whether Stalin's life had really been in danger. My conversations with Nikultsev went on and on, and he called the Kremlin several times in my presence. I thought that this was very serious because after all he came directly from the Kremlin to investigate me. That was his home office. I was sure that he soon became entirely convinced of my innocence.

Nikultsev did something very important for me. I was in love with a high-up NKVD man, Jascha, a member of the Foreign Section who was at that time on a secret mission in Manchuria. I knew he was in Manchuria, and that was not a healthy thing to know. I told Nikultsev that I knew Jascha, and he asked me about him. Then, putting his eyes down (because whenever something is important they look aside) he said, "Well, this information I am going to take with me to Moscow. It's really nobody's business here. It isn't necessary to make a fuss over it, don't mix it up with your affairs, it's better for you," which was very kind of him. It was quite clear that he meant well by this. Among my letters were letters from Jascha, describing Shanghai and the salon of an American literary lady who was apparently the center of this Far

Eastern, underground organization. Her name was Strong.[5][5] All of this was in letters he wrote to me via a friend of his in Paris. [Unbe-knownst to Eva, Fuhlbrügge was interrogated about Jascha on July 20th.]

While Nikultsev was still there, maybe it was in the daytime, or possibly at night, but anyway it was soon after meeting Berman, I was taken in front of a board of about seven people. The center man had a collar with a big star on it. Now, I knew that if you had four rhombuses, you are a general, but if you have a star, you are a marshal. And there were only, I think, five marshals in the whole country. One was Voroshilov, head of the military, one was Budenny, a great general, and there must have been three others, and this was one of them.

Next to the marshal were about six people. I do not remember everything they asked me, but they did ask me about Bykhovskii and what Nikultsev had said. For instance, Nikultsev had asked whether Bykhovskii had any reason to wrong me, and I had told him the anecdote, that mother's cousin, Mr. Seidler, had told me—that if Bykhovskii would have married anyone else it would have been me. So the marshal tried to push me, to convince me that that was why Bykhovskii had wronged me. "Surely you refused his advances." I told the marshal that he had never made any advances. "Surely he must have loved you and he must have…" He tried to make me say that this man had a grudge against me. If it could be shown that he was a jilted lover, the denunciation might not stand. There is a legality, there is a cleanliness, and I was often told that if somebody wrongs you or libels you because he holds a grudge, they accept this as a legal argument for your innocence. But I declined to do this. I was convinced that I had to say the truth. He tried very hard to convince me to say Bykhovskii really had a grudge. But it was not true! I was completely innocent. If I now started to say something that was not true, I might be caught in a net. I never doubted that the best thing was to tell the truth. This is what I had to do.

My accuser had obviously been told he would be shot unless he implicated other people.

Then I went back to Nikultsev. He was not pushing any lies onto me. He seemed to want to get to the truth and get back to Moscow. Perhaps he cared about the truth because this was at the beginning of

---

[5] Eva wasn't sure of this name. It could have been Anna Louise Strong, Mrs. Snow, or Agnes Smedley.

the purges. I mean, later on everybody killed everybody. They gave them a menu of all the leaders; they gave a menu to one of my neighbors in prison and went down the list of the whole Politburo: "This one you wanted to kill? And this one?" But at the time I thought he simply came from the Kremlin to find out if Stalin's life was in danger; he did not want to know anything else. He seemed to be a decent and proper person. I'm sure he was shot. He was too decent not to be shot. He was a very distinguished and nice person. I often thought of him.

After about a week, Nikultsev said he would soon be going back to his office in the Kremlin. In my presence he telephoned for a reservation on the express train to Moscow.

"Why don't you take a ticket for me?" I asked.

He did not answer.

"I have told the investigators here everything I know," he said. "You will have a very hard time and it will last very long. The main thing is the confrontation, because at the confrontation they are going to make up their minds as to who is telling the truth."

"Do you mean this is like a witchcraft trial, that you have to run over hot coals and, depending on whether you burn or not, your innocence is proven?"

He laughed and asked what he could do for me. I told him I was allergic to cold water, and he ordered that I be given a little bit of hot water every day to wash. Then he gave me a newspaper and said, "You must keep your nerves together."

I remember that many, many months later the *korpusnoi*, the little man who picked me up at my last meeting with Nikultsev, mentioned that he remembered Nikultsev giving me the newspaper and speaking to me in German. The *korpusnoi* was a small, simple boy. The other guards called him *zhidovka*, the little Jew, which is not a nice way to put it, not a very proper way to call another korpusnoi. He must have been very much impressed by the way Nikultsev spoke to me because he mentioned it with some respect. Nikultsev had spoken to me as one speaks in the drawing room, and he had wished me well. It was amazing for him to tell me, "You'll have a very hard time. Keep your nerves together; you must keep your nerves together."

Well, Nikultsev had abandoned me. There I was, with the hot water and the newspaper. I did not have any communication with my mother, and was rather scared.

It had a great feeling of unreality. I mean, I was a designer of china; I was not in the business of killing Stalin. This in itself was completely crazy, to put me in a position where I had to defend myself against such a charge. Imagine yourself! It's rather ridiculous. I was completely innocent. I was not even a political person. Alex Weissberg, my husband at the time (but from whom I was already long parted) was a political person. He was critical of the NKVD, and he thought Hitler was not a great asset for the Communist Party—in the beginning, the party line had it that Hitler was a great asset. When Hitler came to power the first slogan was "This is a victory for the Communists," because it was supposed to break down the capitalistic system. Alex had immediately given a speech at the German Club in Kharkov saying that this was a disaster. He had strong opinions and he had made up his mind that Hitler was a disaster. It took quite a long time before the Communist slogan became "Hitler is a disaster." Alex was a political animal—he criticized. I did not criticize. I was completely apolitical. I had come as a tourist to see what was behind the mountain. I was interested in the Communist economy, in how this planned economy worked and how the Russians functioned, but I was not critical at any point. Although Stalin had already started to kill the peasants and *Kulaks*,[6][6] I somehow did not feel strongly about the whole thing, as I did later about the Vietnam war and the Cambodians. At that time I did not have any political side to me.

I am sorry to have to admit this, but all the time I also looked at myself from the outside. You see, most of the time I did not believe that I would have an opportunity to relate this to anybody. I really did not. There was very little probability that I would live—nobody wished me well after Nikultsev had gone. He had had no stake in the matter, and gave me to understand that these other people did have a stake in defending the accusation. But he had abandoned me to "the pack."

---

[6] Kulaks were farmers who, under the Tsar, had worked their way out of the peasantry, to become relatively well off.

My New Interrogator

My new set of investigators was anxious to prove the accusation against me. The "pack" consisted, first of all, of a major. I think I saw the major first with Nikultsev, then several times alone. He was Elias' boss. Elias was to become my personal investigator.

Elias

But the waiting times were a weight to bear—I mean there was very much time between Nikultsev leaving and the arrival of Elias. After a while I did meet Elias, who was to be my investigator for the next six months. His last name was Shmalts and his patronymic was Semenovich. He was tall and good-looking. He came out from behind his desk and reached out his hand to me saying, "I am your investigator. I am 26 years old and I am a lieutenant." That was somehow a source of great pride to him because he was very high up for his 26 years. And so he sat down, and talked to me in a friendly kind of way. He said, "How do you do?" and he meant: "Here I am. I will do everything I can so that you will end up in here for good."

Elias was married. This I knew because later on, when he interrogated me at night, he often called his wife to say he would be late. The fact that he talked to me in a friendly way was part of the act. The act is that he becomes more and more distrustful, and more and more upset about my guilt. In the beginning, he is very friendly, assuming my innocence. Towards the end, many months later, he says, "Don't you see that I have changed my attitude towards you?" But by that time, I was not very shy and said, "But I thought that was part of your act!"

Unfortunately, I do not remember much of the first investigation with Elias. I do not remember what one can talk about for hours. All the other people, they were shouted at, and the shouts sounded like whips! "Fuck your mother!" for hours. I do not know why they said it. I suppose they thought it would induce people to tell the truth. But they did not say it to me. He could not tell me to fuck my mother, I mean, he could not tell me for technical reasons. I did feel physically threatened but fortunately, during the time I was in prison there was no torture. Earlier, they had tortured people in various ways, and later they reintroduced it, but they never physically tortured me. But I knew that they had done it to others. I found out later that the directive for both the halting and the resumption of torture came directly from Stalin.

Throughout the next six months, I saw Elias quite often, usually at night. I do not remember exactly how often. Sometimes I was left stewing for many days. But he did his best to get a confession. Well maybe, now, after many, many years, looking back, maybe he did not do his very best. No, he did not do his best.

What I find so fascinating is that the people who were busy putting me to death were completely nice people. I would have invited them to my home if I had met them in other circumstances. It is still very difficult to understand why these people did it.

Elias had to sign for every shipment of food from my mother, and sometimes for months there was no food from outside. My mother's food packages started to arrive many weeks after my being there. And he also had to sign when I had books, and for maybe a month or six weeks I had no books. I was there alone, with all my troubles, without any books. And it was he who could deprive me of these benefits; he made me very dependent on him.

The way they try to break you is by breaking your dignity. The minute your dignity is gone you are lost. So I made a point of keeping my dignity. Now I am slouching, but when I was opposite him, I was sitting straight. One day his colleague came by and Elias said, "What can I do with her? Look at her, look how she sits!" I mean my dignity was absolutely perfect, and when he asked me what my mother sent in the food packages, I said, "Probably exactly the same as your mother would send you if you would be in my position. Just what mothers send."

One day Elias asked me what I did in prison. I said I wrote poetry. When he asked what ink I used I told him that they gave me cigarettes, matches, and sugar. So I put some cigarette ashes on the sugar and burned it. The ashes helped the sugar to burn and this became a very deep brown molasses.

"And what pen do you use?"

I used the little piece of wood which was sometimes stuck in the kilo of bread. When the bread was not a complete kilo, they attached another piece of bread to it with a little piece of wood. The wood was not very dry so I pulled some threads out of my clothes and, by winding them around it, compressed the wood until it had a very fine point. For paper, I took the wrapping off the cans Mother sent me. (They took the cans out of my cell, but I could keep the wrapping.) And so I wrote letters which were not bigger than a sixteenth of an inch high on this paper. I could write as much as I wanted with these tiny, very clean little letters. Eventually, I memorized the poems, and the papers went down the toilet.

I also had a quill, but it was not a very good quill. I took it out of a pigeon—from its behind. I put some bread in the little opening in the window, and one beautiful day I was sitting there with a pigeon in my hand. I did not know exactly what to do with the pigeon, but I took the feather out of his behind and told him to go out again. So I did have a quill, but it did not help too much because I was not very well acquainted with what to do with quills.

One day they forgot to take a can of something out of my package so I took it out and hid it. Later I took the can with my two hands and tore it into pieces, which is very difficult. I kept one of these small pieces in my shoe. I do not know what I did with the rest, but after that, I kept this "knife" with me all the time. Occasionally, my mother sent an apple. I could peel this apple with my teeth so that the whole spiral stayed absolutely intact, which alarmed the guards greatly because how could I do that without a knife? When I came out, I still had the knife in my shoe.

My Feelings

What were my feelings? First of all, you are in a cage, you are suddenly in a cage, in a dark gray-green cage, without any books, without anything to do, with very, very many hours, very many minutes, very many seconds of gruesome, dumb depression. You cannot survive if you say, "This is a mistake. I must be released!" You cannot. You cannot. You can only survive by saying, "I have closed my life. I have had a wonderful time, but I have nowhere to go from here." You have to. I was twenty-nine and a half.

You cannot survive the skipping girl looking at the sun; you cannot if your heart breaks. You can only survive if you have given up all hope of everything in the future. You can only live with total resignation. Very soon, you have to accept this attitude. You cannot think of your mother, you cannot think of a pussycat, you cannot think of a child, you cannot think of anything in your recent past. And there is no future. You can think of your long-ago past, or speak French to yourself. Nikultsev warned me: "This will take a very long time." Here I was in this cage. It is terrible to be in a cage. It is very hard to live. It is very hard to eat, it is very hard to make pee-pee and it is all very, very hard. Everything is artificial. You force yourself to do all these things. You can feel neither injustice nor hope. I had no reason to believe that I would ever get out. I had every reason to believe that this was the end. This was absolutely the end. Out of the sixteen months, ten were without hope.

Daily Routine

Let me tell you about my daily routine. First of all, you were not permitted to lie down on the bed. You could not even sit on the bed. If you lay down, they would immediately come and tell you to get up. You could only sit on the little, metal, fold-down shelf next to the table. You went to bed at 9:00 at night. At seven in the morning, they opened up the little wicket in the door and said, "Give me your spoon." And into the spoon they ladled two little spoonfuls of sugar, and then the next person came and into your little aluminum cup they poured tea. They just opened the door and said, "Your cup," or "Your spoon." I had an aluminum bowl, an aluminum mug, and a wooden spoon, a carved Russian spoon, with a narrow handle and a round bowl. I put the wooden spoon through the opening and she ladled two teaspoons of sugar into it. Then the tea came from a huge teakettle, and a block— one kilo—of dark, sour, moist bread.

There was a way to call the attendant. I forget what it was. When you needed toilet paper, she came and gave you a small square of brown paper. From a newspaper, you could have derived interesting information, but this was just a small piece of wrapping paper.

I did have a toothbrush. Some people had their toothbrush taken away (you can use it for choking), but I had a toothbrush to clean my teeth, and then I brushed my hair and washed my face. The sink and the toilet were both in the cell; it was a very fine prison. After about three weeks, one of the guards, the skinny one, said, "Your bowl is not very shiny. Wash your bowl better." When I asked what I should wash it with, she said (in Russian), "With human bone." In English, you would say "elbow grease," but I did not know that, so I swallowed and said, "All right, give me some." You see, I had the feeling that once my fellow prisoners had died their bones were ground up for me to wash my bowl with! After all, if that is the custom…

Then I would do gymnastics. You can stand on your head—that you can do on the bed—and bicycle with your feet. That is very good. Once when I was standing on my head, bicycling with my legs to get some well-being, the guard, the second youngest one, opened the peephole and said, "Your arms look as if they were turned out of wood." That was Russian. She opened it just to say that my arms were beautiful.

Then came lunch. At lunchtime there was often a soup, mostly a cabbage soup with a little bit of potato and meat at the bottom. As I became an older and older inmate, and as they became fonder and fonder of me because I had been there the longest, they gave me two or three of these aluminum bowls. When they had fed everybody, they came back and put what was left in the bottom of the soup bucket in the three bowls, so I could separate the cabbage from the potato and from the juice. That gave me three separate portions, which was very elegant. Then there was this gooey sort of kasha, which was really the same thing people ate every day, this buckwheat kasha, but it was boiled to a grayish sort of mush. With the kilo of bread, plus the mush filling up the aluminum bowl, it was certainly enough; you did not get hungry. Sometimes instead of this mush, we got another yellowish sort of grain, but not very often. From time to time, we had a fish soup, which consisted of very nourishing salmon fat, eyes and heads; it was obviously given to us after the hospitals or other institutions had gotten the rest of the fish. It was full of fish fat, with these big eyes floating around, many big eyes. That could not be eaten. That was too much.

And at the beginning, I had the newspaper, so after lunch I sat down to read the newspaper. The one Nikultsev had given me had lasted a long time, six months. I can tell you what was in the newspaper: there was one article about the Armenians. They began to endear themselves to me more and more because they had kept the Greek philosophers for us in their monasteries during the Middle Ages. Then there was— there must have been one more newspaper because all that could not have been in one newspaper—there was the draft of the new Russian constitution, which I knew by heart because it was in this newspaper. I had learned Russian mostly from a dictionary with a little grammar in the back, and I had memorized a great deal.

After reading this newspaper, I would walk from one corner of my cell to the other, quite a bit, most systematically. Six and a half paces diagonally. Then I composed poems, trying to fill the time, to eat up the time. Most of my poems had a cadence to the six and a half paces. If I tell you one, you will hear it. It was always this way, you see, six and one-half steps take me to the end of a line.

There is so much time to be eaten up, to be consumed without despairing, that you get tired. It is very hard work, so you get exhausted. When I came out, I was terribly tired. First of all, you cannot consume time without killing it with thoughts. It is constantly being filled with some thought. These thoughts are produced on purpose. It is not that they wander in and out. You cannot permit thoughts to wander because there are certain thoughts you must keep away from. You cannot just think of your mother, for instance. It is impossible. You must think of something else. And it is a constant effort. And then, of course, your feeling of time changes. Because when I came out, I hardly started on a thought and it was already midday. That means suddenly time changed. Prison time, alone in a cell, without books for many months, is a different sort of time. You are happy to have one thought in an hour and a half. Then the time was well filled; you had had a good day.

One of my thoughts involved constructing a bra. I knew how it would be sewn and designed and constructed, and that made a very, very good day because it was so well filled.

I had had another very good thought. Just before I was arrested I was given half of a room as my own living space. I received it from the Commissar because I had worked so well. The room was still whole when I saw it but it was supposed to be cut in half. And I thought about how to make a very elegant party in such a room, how one would come in, where who would sit, and I furnished this entire room. I do not really remember many of the other thoughts, but they were either a poem or had very definite content. The main thing was to have a good and productive day and to prevent your heart from dropping.

I also played chess with myself, or *mühle*, making little square tic-tac-toes out of the pieces of the kneadable, soft bread. I was not in control of who won. I could say which side I wanted to win, but I always won in spite of myself!

And then there was the sunshine. I had the sunshine from here to there, and then it disappeared. Well, that made it kind of cheerful, because it was very dreary otherwise.

Every third day I was taken for a seven-minute walk in the courtyard. The guard stood in one corner and I walked in a circle. Every ten days they took me down the hall for a shower. In the shower, someone had scratched the name "Pushkin," and I was touched to see the national hero remembered here.

During my first summer in prison, by craning my neck to see over the metal shield on my window, I watched a young guard quarreling with his wife on a fire escape high above the courtyard. The next summer their baby was sunning itself and they had stopped quarreling.

I must tell you that sometimes one has great worries (one has very often great worries, and rightly so), and then they did give you valerian drops. You put out your spoon and they put a little of this brown juice into it. It's a tranquilizer. They cannot give it you constantly, but they are permitted to give it to you.

The day in which you wash your cell is a very good day. One of my neighbors once told me through the crack around the water faucet that she was terribly depressed, and I said, "Wash your floor from one corner to the other. It will do you a heap of good!"

In the evening, the little wicket opened again and someone said, "Pass your bowl," and there was soup. Then, at nine o'clock, the light went on for the night and one went to sleep, unless one was taken out for a nighttime interrogation.

The Guards

There were two male guards, called korpusnoi, and several women guards. One of the korpusnoi was a big fellow, the other, the small Jew, who at the very end of my sixteen months, when I was being sent out of the country, said to me, "You will be back. You'll see. The times will change. All this will change. You will be back."

Of the women guards, one was an old, roundish sort, one was very thin, and one was a middle-young girl. It was the latter who said to me, "This job is all so educating, so educating." She was about twenty-five and very soft. She once poured out her heart to me, telling me of her terrible troubles, not noticing that mine were so much greater.

The guards were permitted to give you things, but absolutely forbidden to take anything out of the cell under threat of being put into prison themselves. That meant that they could give you cigarettes or matches of their own, but could never accept any.

All of the guards seemed completely neutral. None of them was mean or rough, at least to me.

Fellow Prisoners

For sixteen months, I lived in cell number four. During that time, I had many neighbors, even some roommates. My first neighbor, in number five, seemed to be a perfectly sober person. I had talked to her originally through the faucet, which I had jiggled enough to be able to talk through and also to smell through. Whenever somebody new came into number five, I always knew because she had perfumed soap and this perfumed soap could be smelled through the carefully jiggled faucet.

So this first neighbor was a very normal person, a dentist, I think, from Arkhangelsk, and a Social Revolutionary. But after some time, she started to repeat on and on and on: "Shtolanya … what evil did I do, what terrible thing did I do?" When somebody came into her cell, I heard him say, "Why do you bite your hands? They are bloody, why do you bite your hands?" She was obviously completely gone. She was punishing herself by biting her knuckles, repeating over and over, "What did I do?" Then a man came in and said, "Well, if you committed a crime…" pretending that he thought she had done something wrong. But what she had really done, she told me later, was to accuse innocent people. Apparently, she just gave up and nodded yes to everyone they asked about. They were all arrested, and she went off her rocker.

My neighbor in number three tried to commit suicide by hanging herself. Her name was Natasha, and she was accused of belonging to a "social group." Someone had involved the rest of the group by saying something that by law had to be denounced, and by not denouncing this person everybody was now involved and was open to blackmail. It was quite clear to me that at that time there was German activity in Russia, and that was the type of group she belonged to.

I had already taught Natasha how to knock on the wall so we could "talk" to each other. How did I know about knocking? From two sources. I had seen it in a Russian movie showing how the old revolutionaries knocked on the prison walls to communicate with each other—they had shown the grid and the letters—and the same grid was engraved on the wall of the shower. I saw it in the shower and I think that reminded me of the movie.

I saw Natasha only once, on the way to the shower. When you walked somewhere there was a guard in front and a guard behind you. As you went down the hallway, the guards knocked on the walls to announce their coming; when you passed another prisoner you had to turn away. But I still saw her. She was a very tall, blonde girl with straight braids, completely straight blonde braids, down to her ankles.

After Natasha tried to hang herself, they came into her cell to cut her down and I heard her shout and cry. Much later I knocked to find out what had happened. We always said only the beginnings of words. Whenever a word is already understood you knocked quickly a few times, because it is a very long process to make a whole word. So I said, knocking, "I heard you shout and cry 'They beat me!'" She answered. I knocked back, saying that I thought they had cut off her braids. When she asked why, I said, "Because they're so practical to hang yourself with." She knocked immediately: "Ha, ha, ha." Laughing through the wall like this was very funny. That was Natasha.

When Natasha was being cut down, the girl in number six shouted through the whole cellblock, "Don't get the korpusnoi, get a doctor!" Number six was always indignant. Of course, one had every reason to be indignant to the utmost degree; there was injustice in every cell. But one could not be indignant without going crazy. Finally, I did hear number six being dragged out on the floor. Number six must have been a young girl.

Of course, there was somebody in number two and one, but I did not know who they were. In number five I knew several people, three at least. One was Galina, a young married woman. I saw her once when she was being taken to the shower and my little peephole was not completely closed—there was a little moon left open. She had short hair. She was a very young, very nice girl, nice family. Galina had gone to the German school (there was a German school just as there were French schools) and her husband was a hydroelectric engineer. At that time a great percentage of hydroelectric engineers were being arrested. And she, poor girl, said she knew that her husband belonged to a Russian fascist organization that was connected to the German embassy, and that anytime the boss came in she was sent out of the room. But it was certainly not a counter-revolutionary organization, she continued. Her husband had told her it was a revolutionary organization, so why were they accusing her of being a counter-revolutionary? And I said, "My dear, against whom was this revolution?" I do not know why she did not know what her husband was doing.

There is no doubt that there was a fifth column organized by the German embassies—other people doubt it, but I know it. I had other inklings of it later too, but there is no doubt that this was one of them. It was always the Germans who started such groups, and her husband was the leader of this one. She did not know what Fascism was. She was completely apolitical. When her husband told her, "This is a revolutionary organization," she could not have cared less. She was very young.

Through the faucet, Galina and I developed a great friendship. She got the books I recommended, with very good menus, the best menus you could find. Dickens always had very good things to eat, so had Gogol, so had Cellini. After a while, we talked in Cellini's terms: "I have a dagger that I will push through your heart," and such things. We never discussed sex (I was completely frigid when I came out), but we did not mind indulging in food. We read about it with great pleasure. The longer the menus, the better the book!

Then I told her what Fascism was. I had a book there by Kronin, a history of the Party. The prison librarian had left it with me for my instruction—until one day he retrieved it with great alarm, as in the meantime it had been declared dangerously counter-revolutionary. So out of this book I gave her the definition of Fascism, which is "the last, upswing of the dying capitalism, in its most violent form," or something of this sort. I read this to her through the faucet and she answered, "*Evichka, kakaia umnitsa*...what a clever little one you are to know these things." But after this, she was told she was going to be put in a much worse prison. Ours was really a very good prison, it had a toilet, it was more or less clean. So before she left, she came to the faucet and said, "Eva Alexandrovna, you will be my lightest memory throughout my life," and then she left. That was Galina.

Then there was another woman who sang Offenbach. She was not there long; she was a very high-up Party functionary. You were not supposed to sing or to whistle, you were not to make any noise, except giving your name when the guard came to take you out. That was all. You were not supposed even to hum a song. But she did. She sang Offenbach, *Orpheus In The Underworld*, or *La Belle Hélène*. That is what she hummed all the time before she was taken away.

She was arrested for having guaranteed an affidavit. The rule was that anybody who guaranteed for anybody else got the same prison sentence. Here was a high Party functionary who had stood up for someone else. She knew she was facing her trial that night. There is no real trial, of course. At midnight, there are people sitting there and they say you are either to be shot or sentenced to ten years labor, or whatever, but I did not think she would be shot. There she was humming these Offenbach tunes, very gently, very quietly, and very sweetly, and I asked her if she did not want to think about her case— about her defense? She said she had vouched for someone, so there was nothing to think about, and she continued singing, deep into the night until she was taken away.

So my neighbors in the Leningrad prison were the dentist from Arkhangelsk who went crazy, Natasha, and Galina, and the party functionary. During the time of Galina, I had a roommate for four months who was my scourge.

She was my scourge because of her complete idiocy, she was so stupid. Actually, she was a nurse. Once Galina said to her through the faucet, "Don't be so desperate. You are a nurse. You will get into a Russian camp. There are the most interesting people in the camps." This girl had also gone to the German school, and one day she came back from her investigation and said that the investigator had told her something she could never repeat, it was so horrible and it was just terrible what they did to people here. I told her to try to repeat it and she whispered: "*Donnerwetter!*" That means "thunder-weather." It is as if you would say, "Darn it!" in English.

She was so pompous and stupid that I could not resist educating her—a bit upside down—like telling her that Hamlet was a musical and Africa a mountain. I told her all sorts of wrong things. I forgot what else I told her. She just irritated me no end with her pompous stupidity. She was very religious, and when I asked what language Jesus spoke, she said, "Of course, Old Church Russian!" I told her many things, so she left well-educated.

And then there was this prostitute in my cell. She was there only six or seven days. She said that before she had been arrested, she had taken her silk Shantung to a seamstress somewhere out of town to be made into a blouse, and that this seamstress and her husband were old aristocrats, or something, who always turned on Hitler's speeches when she came in. This was, of course, forbidden. She had met someone there (or perhaps it was they themselves) who was related to the doorman at the German embassy. So I met this German embassy, and its various feelers, several different times. She constantly complained about the loss of the silk Shantung blouse. But she wanted to use the time very well, so she asked me how foreigners make love. She wanted to know all about it because she knew that there was much to be learned. She was an industrious professional and wanted to know everything. And I am not really going to tell you all she told me, but she did give me some very important advice.

When we had nothing to do, my prostitute roommate and I tried to see how many different types of dogs each of us knew, St. Bernard, dachshund, etc. We had to move the time somehow. But then she started to say, "Well, Stalin is really terrible, oughtn't he be killed?" or some such thing. To this I said, "I'll call the guard if you don't shut up." She was just a very stupid agent provocateur, I think, because later I noticed her washing the floor outside the cell, which meant that she was a criminal, not a political prisoner. She was definitely put in with me as an agent provocateur. Well, I do not know exactly how subtle she was, but it was quite clear that she was there for this purpose.

I had the prostitute for six or eight days, and the nurse about four months and that was all there was for the next six months. For all but the last few days of the last six months of my imprisonment, I was not only alone, but nobody talked to me. I was not called out. Actually, I was not quite alone:

Just before the end, a lovely, high-spirited German girl was put in with me. She had worked as a Russian spy in Hitler's Germany. She was careful not to disturb the spider web spanning my cell, which I had protected for so long. She somehow understood that my life hung by this thread.

During these months of solitary confinement I had much time to write poems.

A Package from my mother

My mother and I had talked about an acquaintance who had been arrested long before me, who had become phlegmatic after only six months. Clearly my mother wanted to avoid this by amusing me by sending packages. Mother, who was a historian and in no way a housewife, started to bake tens of different sorts of fine, little cookies, including in each package a great variety, with vanilla, with nuts, with God knows what. The other things she sent me were also rather extraordinary, such as crab meat. Always very full of imagination. Once or twice I got a reasonable package, a package like one would imagine a package to be—some cheese, some sausage, some this and that. Only my sister-in-law or my brother could make such a down to earth, normal package. It didn't have any of her flavor, and therefore I broke into deep depression, thinking that it showed that something had happened to Mother. But then, again, came her usual packages, full of charm and loveliness.

While the prostitute was still in my cell, I got one of my mother's food packages and she said, "My God! Look at all these *tchotchkes*?" That was the first time I heard the word tchotchkes. She might have been a Jewish prostitute, I do not know. Anyway, she had picked up this word somewhere. The package had powdered Jello, which was a great sensation because it was new to the guards. They wanted very much to see how it jelled. My mother also sent something I mixed; I think it was cocoa and butter, so I made a kind of chocolate filling with my sugar and chocolate cream.

I had the feeling that my mother and I were so close that she would send me whatever I wanted. So I told my prostitute roommate that if she desired anything, she just had to tell me and I would order it. She said she wanted cauliflower and, sure enough, in the next package, or the one afterwards, there was a tiny, complete, two-inch bud of cauliflower! And I said, "See? You ordered it. Here it is!" But, of course, this was cauliflower season and, quite naturally, mother thought that that would be a nice thing to send.

When Mother had no money, she sent me mayonnaise, and I ate the mayonnaise on black bread. I still love mayonnaise and I still, secretly, eat mayonnaise on bread. The mayonnaise label described the foods it was supposed to go with—that was the great upswing in culture for food in the Soviet Union. So there were ten different kinds of mayonnaise. One was to go with crab meat and others with other fine foods. When times were bad I got just the mayonnaise, and had to imagine the foods it was supposed to accompany. When times were better, depending on what my brother gave her for money, she sent me crab meat itself.

After some months, my investigator Elias Semenovich gave me a card and said I could write to my mother. I sent a message to her saying that my life was in danger, something she did not know, could not know. I did it by writing the little card full, and then, down at the corner, putting: "Because of lack of space I cannot write anymore." This referred to a dream I had discussed with her just before I was arrested. I had dreamt that somebody killed me because of lack of space. I thought she might understand that I am in terrible danger if I used the same phrase. On that card I asked her to send me warm woolen underpants (although it was July), a pillow, and lemon extract to make lemonade. The next package had lemon crystals in it, woolen underpants and a pillowcase. Not a pillow, but a pillowcase. I was convinced that she had gotten my card and that now she knew what it was about. I only found out later that she had not gotten my card, it was just that she always knew what I wanted.

Another time she included a photograph of my little niece Michelle, the baby whom I had left when she was two months old. Now she had a fur hat on and was smiling. It was a real baby, a real child. As usual, the korpusnoi, the man who was chief of this cell block, delivered the package to me. Although I was always very controlled, when I opened it, and saw the picture of this baby, I broke into tears for the first time. Tears were just gushing out of my eyes and pain gripped my heart, physically gripped my heart. I had rejected all thoughts of children and animals, of things which were warming and which were close to life, and this brought it back to me. It made me soft, completely soft.

Much later, when I came out, Hans [Zeisel] asked me whether it wouldn't have been a great comfort to have had a kitten. I looked at him in amazement. A kitten would have killed me. The only way for me to survive these months of hopelessness and worry was to detach myself from any soft feeling, to keep myself aloof from sentiment and warmth. Had I had a cat I would have gone mad. I could not have controlled myself. Self-pity would have overcome me. I would have gone off my rocker like the people to the left and right of me. When I came out I was completely frigid emotionally.

The Second Accusation

Although the first six months, June to December, 1936, while these roommates and neighbors were going in and out of my life, Elias Semenovich continued to do his best to have me confess to the original accusation: that I had planned to kill Stalin. That was his business, trying to convince me. But now they were preparing a second, different accusation, which I found out about by accident. I was saved from this second accusation by a coincidence that I consider a miracle. Before describing the miracle, let me tell you something I found out much later, which put these accusations into a broader, more understandable political framework.

Orlov's Book

In the 1950s, I found a book in the New York Public Library called *The Secret History of Stalin's Crimes*, by Alexander Orlov.[7] In it I saw several things which applied to myself. I could tell that the book was written by someone very much on the inside of the NKVD because whatever I knew about it was absolutely true.

The first point was connected to my friend Jascha, the NKVD man who at that time was in Manchuria, and whom Nikultsev had warned me not to mention. Jascha had been an investigator in the Menshevik accusations in 1931. The prisoner he interrogated, an old Bolshevik, was a man whom he greatly respected and knew to be innocent. When, after some time, Jascha had no false confession to show for his efforts, his superior ordered him to use forceful method, and gave a demonstration, having the poor, dignified older man climb up and down the stairs on his knees until he fainted from exhaustion.

Orlov said it was Stalin, dissatisfied with the failure of the investigators to obtain confessions from their "Menshevik" prisoners, who gave the order: "Mount your prisoner and do not unmount him until he has given you the testimony!" This meant torture.

Disgusted, Jascha refused to torture his prisoner and soon found himself in prison. From his cell he watched for six months as his cellmates were led out to be shot, no one knowing who was next.

---

[7] Orlov, Alexander. The Secret History of Stalin's Crimes, p. 63, (New York: Random House, 1953).

After six months, Jascha was "rehabilitated" and put in charge of a not-very-important agricultural office. A short time after his release he attended the trial of the old man.

According to Orlov's book, in 1936, when preparations began for the show trial that Bykhovskii and I were to be a part of, Yagoda, head of the NKVD, issued a circular forbidding the use of violence, threats and promises.[8][8] But later, when the investigators were not getting enough confessions, Molchanov, then in charge of the investigations, told them, "I am telling you officially, in the name of the People's Commissar [Yagoda], go back to your prisoners and give them the works. Mount your prisoners and don't unmount them until they have given you the testimony." Orlov writes that everyone knew who had actually authored this terrible phrase.

Several months after my arrest, I first heard the shouts of the girl from cell number six, and I knew that the use of torture had begun again.

Also, in Orlov's book, I found a reference to my accuser, Bykhovskii. Orlov wrote that there had been an NKVD man in the Russian trade commission in Germany, a Latvian citizen named Valentin Olberg, who was groomed to give false testimony against some higher-ups. Olberg was to be a "fictitious defendant" in the first Moscow show trial. (A "fictitious defendant" was someone planted by the NKVD, whose purpose was to incriminate the other defendants.) He was brought back to Russia and given a professorship in Gorky, which he thought was a great promotion.

Then, according to Orlov, Olberg was arrested and told "Now look, you worked at this Trade Commission, and there were these higher-ups. They are all spies, and you will do us a great favor if you would say that you knew they were spies," or something of this sort.

He signed everything against these "enemies," after which they continued, saying, "You also have to involve some people you know better. What about your friends? What about your relatives?"

Olberg didn't want to sign a deposition against his close friends. So they said, "All right, then we will put you into a basement, or shoot you," or something of this sort, whereupon he signed a deposition against his friends, including his Latvian friend, Bykhovskii, who had been an engineer in the Lomonosov china factory where I had worked.

---

[8] Ibid. p. 60.

(Bykhovskii was then accused of making certain bombs, but it was impossible that he could have done that, so the bomb-making disappeared from the accusation.) But once Bykhovskii was brought in, it was quite clear that they said to him: "Here is this deposition of your dear friend, that you belong to this organization. Who else did you bring into this organization? We will shoot you if you don't tell us. Who are the foreigners you worked with?" So he gave the name of several friends and relatives, and of the two foreigners he had worked with, namely me and my modelmaker, Fuhlbrügge.

Much of this I learned later. The book only gives Bykhovskii's name. Orlov writes:

> But in the unpublished depositions signed by Olberg in the NKVD, which I read in Moscow, I saw several more names of his friends whom he was ordered to slander. Among them I remember well...Bykhovskii.[9]

Now here is the third connection I found. It is almost too improbable to believe. Orlov continues:

> In the middle of May 1936, an important conference took place in the Kremlin at which Stalin, Yezhov, and Yagoda [were] present. The conference was entirely devoted to the analysis of the accusations that had been fabricated against Trotsky. Knowing with what exceptional attention Stalin approached everything that concerned Trotsky, [an aide] prepared ... a special diagram ... of the "terrorist conspiracy"...After Stalin had heard the reports of the investigation chiefs, he drew their attention to the fact that that he did not see in the whole outline of the conspiracy a single prisoner who would testify that he had been [a courier] sent to the Soviet Union by Trotsky for the purpose of committing a terrorist act.[10]

And lo and behold, that was exactly the accusation against me, which I would overhear a short time after this meeting in the Kremlin.

The Miracle

A t night in the summer, one heard, like whips going all night long, "Fuck your mother! Fuck your mother! Fuck your mother!" It went all

---

[9] Ibid. p. 65.
[10] Ibid. p. 107.

through the night. When this "Fuck your mother" started, you could hear the bang, bang, bang of the windows being shut. You could not take listening to that all night long.

Everyone closed his window, but on this one night, I did not close my window, and this is what I consider a miracle: Suddenly I heard my name. I was in cell number four. There were two more cells in the cellblock, five and six. Then came a wall, at ninety degrees, making the second side of the courtyard, and this investigation must have been going on behind this other wall, about one flight above me, near an open window.

So as the fly flies it was not more than thirty feet from me. All night long I heard this investigation. It started with a rude investigator who must have had an assistant, because all through the night I heard him say, "Write! Write! Write!" as if he had someone taking things down for him. Bykhovskii's investigator, Migbert, was the only one I had ever met who had an assistant. I recognized the voice. It was Migbert, a brutal, ugly man who had gotten the first deposition against me from Bykhovskii, and who was now getting a second one from this fellow upstairs.

The accused man was asked, "What did you do?"

He said, "I was a Trotskyite."

"How long have you been a Trotskyite?"

"Since, I don't know, twenty years."

"You're freezing? You will be even colder!"

It was summer. Why was he freezing? This meant that before the investigation, he had obviously been held in a cold basement.

And then, after awhile, the investigator said, "Have you contacted Trotsky?"

"Yes."

"Who brought you the news from Trotsky? Who brought you the information from Trotsky?"

There was no answer. Then the investigator shouted, "And Eva Alexandrovna Stricker?"

My name! The investigator was giving him my name! And the accused answered, "I don't know her, I don't know her!"

"Don't cover up!" shouted the investigator—he must have been standing next to the window because I heard him so clearly—"We will destroy her anyway. We have enough. Your deposition makes no difference."

I did not know this man, and he did not know me. The investigator repeated, "We will destroy her anyway. Your deposition makes no difference; we have enough. Don't cover up for her, don't, don't!"

This beautiful thing went on all through the night, with "Fuck your mother! Fuck your mother! Fuck your mother!" and so on. And here I was listening to my name shouted through the night, "Eva Alexandrovna Stricker!" It went on and on and on. Finally, towards morning, the accused said, "I want my glasses." He wanted to read what he was signing. "You don't need your glasses. Sign!" It was my impression that he signed.

Now I was faced with what to do. A day or two earlier my investigator, Elias Semenovich, had asked me where I had spent my vacations. I had said in Paris, and I do not know where—Austria, Italy, and again in Paris. One of the things I had heard through the courtyard during the night was, "Don't you know Trotsky lives in Paris? Don't you know Eva Alexandrovna was in Paris? Don't you know that she went to Paris and back as a courier?"

So, the next day, promptly, I was called out and this time Elias asked, "Did you spend your vacation in Paris?" I answered, "Partly," and he said, "Sign in the margin." My investigator could prove the man's confession merely by asking, "Were you in Paris?" The last time he had asked about my trips he had not taken any notes. But on this day, the day after the overhead nighttime investigation, he made a very official transcript and, each time it said I was in Paris, he said, "Sign in the margin." So I had very clear proof to myself that there was a deposition against me saying that I was Trotsky's courier from Paris.

That was the second accusation. The first accusation was that I wanted to kill Stalin. I was as dead as a doornail. You could not have been any deader than having two depositions against you.

According to Orlov, at just about this time Stalin had "requested" a courier from Trotsky in order to prove the "conspiracy" against him. So whether this was a total war between Mr. Stalin, personally, and me, I do not know. But when I read the book, it gave me the shivers because it seemed to me a very close connection.

After Elias's investigation, in which I signed "in the margins," I was brought back home to my cell and I started to think what to do. I did not function immediately.

I decided to accuse the investigation of using illegal methods. You know, everything had to be very clean and legal in these things. I should not have heard the investigation against me. The fact that I did hear it was not a clean thing. It had been badly botched; it was an absolute mess. So, I decided to accuse my accusers. I asked to see my investigator, Elias Semenovich.

Accusing The Accusers

As I entered, I could see that Elias's face was white. He handed me a paper signed by the supervisor of the building where I had once stayed and two other people, swearing that two revolvers were found among my possessions. I knew that this was fabricated, as I did not have any revolvers.

When I was arrested, as I wrote earlier, I told them that I had some more things in the maid's room where I had lived before moving in with my brother and his family. The house belonged to a Hungarian revolutionary who was at the time a high Party functionary in Russia. He and his wife had kindly let me use their maid's room until I got my own room. It was very small, but I had stored several things in it including a sewing machine, the same sewing machine that is now in my attic. It was there that they had supposedly found the revolvers.

Up to now Elias did not really believe I was guilty, but as he handed me this paper I could see he was shaken. There was the paper that said that two revolvers had been found in my sewing machine by the supervisor of this building and two other people. I saw that Elias was scared. He did not want me to have two revolvers. If somebody is accused of wanting to kill Stalin, and has two revolvers in her sewing machine, it is rather bad. When the paper was presented to me I immediately got diarrhea, not five minutes later, but the same second, and I said to Elias, "Please, I have to go to the bathroom." I reacted physically.

There were now two different, deadly accusations, plus two revolvers. One accusation was that I wanted to kill Stalin, the other that I was a Trotskyite courier. I mean, that's not very healthy. The revolvers did not please me either. I knew I had no revolvers, and I could not believe that they would let a foreigner out of the country with the specific knowledge that the NKVD works with false evidence.

"But you wanted to see me," he said. "You wanted to tell me something. What is it you wanted to tell me?" I shrugged my shoulders and said, "It's not worth it anymore." After he had shown me the false affidavits about the revolvers, I thought nothing could help me, so I said, "I have nothing to tell you anymore." I gave up.

I was returned to my cell. By this time, I had already lived for a long time without hope, still expecting the confrontation with Bykhovskii at any time, and fully expecting to be shot. It would have been irresponsible to deceive myself with false optimism. I was living a perfectly artificial daily life. I did not live because of my instincts, but because I thought it was unfair to Mother to kill myself. I had resolved, however, that if I were still in prison two years later, I would certainly do everything to kill myself.

I had already eliminated any thought that there would be a future. This feeling stayed with me long after I came out. Years later, if someone said, well, in September we go there—or let us meet next Thursday—or even two days hence, I laughed inside and thought, This has no reality for me whatsoever! There never will be a two days hence; there never will be a next month. It was like saying let's meet on the moon! But each day that came was an unexpected surprise, and I greeted it happily.

From the moment I had been put in prison, my whole world, all my relationships and points of reference had changed. This had been such a total, unexpected change that it is hard to comprehend. Everything was so absurd that each time something happened, I had to rearrange the reference points of my life. If I was going to be shot before my thirtieth year, that would obviously be the end of my life, and I had to shift the middle of my life to when I was fifteen. This is not quite so easy, rearranging one's whole life. But, whenever you die, life is concluded as a whole. And when I looked back, I had the feeling—yes, I did live well and it was worthwhile.

I knew that the confrontation and my subsequent death could come at any moment. I had the unappetizing image of my body as a soon-to-be rotting thing. I looked at my hands and feet. I looked at the reflection of my face in the toilet, and considered my head as a thing, yellow and decaying. This is hard to imagine, but it had become my daily concern, my daily relationship to my own body.

I also wondered about the procedure of being shot. I knew that one was shot in the back of the head, and hoped that one was dead immediately. But if not, is one left to die? I also was very curious about the smell. Would it smell like disinfectant, or would it smell like blood when one goes to be shot? This was not an abstract or even a morbid thought. It was logical to think of these things.

I had been considering them for a long time when suddenly I was led to the confrontation. This was shortly after the revolver affidavit. I am quite sure now, although I do not remember exactly, that I was not told ahead of time when the confrontation was going to take place. One of the tricks of their trade is to surprise you at every point. But on the other hand, I am sure I was preparing for it, because by that time I had been told a great many details of when and where I was supposed to have met Bykhovskii. Almost every detail in these accusations was wrong—I had not been in those places and I did not meet him at those times. So in this respect I was quite well prepared.

I knew that this was what Nikultsev had referred to as the most important moment of the examination. In the confrontation room, Bykhovskii was sitting on a chair, facing three people behind a desk: Elias Semenovich; Migbert, Bykhovskii's rude, ugly investigator and, Migbert's secretary. My chair was not very far from Bykhovskii, and also faced the table.

There is something wrong with my recollection of the details of the confrontation. I think what is wrong is that I felt a puzzling, incongruous lightheartedness throughout the proceedings and also afterwards, hours after I returned to my cell. It was totally illogical and contradictory given the reality of what happened.

I do not remember who read the long accusation, which was allegedly in Bykhovskii's words. From time to time, he was asked whether the words were correct, and he nodded. Every few sentences I was asked to respond, and each time I said, "I was not there, I could not have been there. These conversations could not have taken place."

I had been quite somewhere else. Neither the place nor the time fit. "It doesn't matter whether the place or the time fits," Migbert, Bykhovskii's investigator shouted, "You had these conversations and that's that!"

I had only a side view of Bykhovskii during all of this, but I felt that he occasionally glanced at me. And then I noticed what in my memory stands out as the most remarkable aspect of the entire confrontation: on the side of his nostril was a huge, protruding, white pimple that culminated in a black point. And it hit me with great and deep disgust that he was going to be shot and become a dead body with this huge blackhead on his nose, of which he seemed to be totally oblivious.

It is difficult to realize how acutely one feels the prospect of being dead. I had no doubt that Bykhovskii would soon be shot, because I had no doubt then that he was guilty. After all, he admitted in his accusation against me that he was a violent, active enemy of the system, a Trotskyite and a spy. It did not occur to me that the truth was that this poor fellow was as innocent as I, and had been forced into doing this.

At one point, I apparently became nervous and wanted a cigarette, and Bykhovskii took out a pack and offered me one. I remember almost shuddering at the idea taking a cigarette from the hand of a dead body.

The master of ceremonies of the confrontation was Migbert, Bykhovskii's loud, furious, efficient investigator. When the deposition came to the point that I had prepared the revolvers to shoot Stalin, and invited my modelmaker from Berlin to be the sharpshooter, he stood up, waved the papers in the air and shouted: "Here is the accusation and here are the revolvers. The chickens must laugh at your denial!"

They had even inserted a few German phrases into the deposition to make it seem more authentic. When Bykhovskii had allegedly asked me: "With what will you shoot Stalin?" I was supposed to have replied in German: "und was die Waffen betrift is alles in Ordnung." [Concerning the weapons, everything is in order.]

Now came the strange reaction: I was neither sad, nor burdened, nor worried. I was extremely, surprisingly, lighthearted. I said quietly, "If you have decided to kill me, there is nothing I can do to prevent it."

When it was over, I suppose to the great satisfaction of Bykhovskii's investigator (I do not remember Elias saying a single word during this procedure), I was led out and kept in some sort of waiting room. Sometime later I was taken to my cell. No sooner had I arrived in my cell than I was taken back to the waiting room, where I was kept for quite a long time before again being taken back to my cell. I never found out why. Perhaps they had wanted to ask me more questions, and then changed their minds.

My cozy, lightheartedness continued after returning to my cell. I felt I had done very well, that everything was fine. Actually, the opposite was the case. Everything was terrible. Much later I wondered whether something had happened in my head, out of fear, that paralyzed my emotions, preventing me from feeling more pain and being more scared, or whether it is possible that I was drugged. I am absolutely sure that I was not normal on this occasion. I did not feel what I was supposed to feel. I did not feel fear. I felt almost happy.

Elias's Trip to Moscow

Shortly after the confrontation an amazing thing happened: Elias left Leningrad and went to Moscow to find out two things: information about my modelmaker, Fuhlbrügge (whether I had known him previously or not), and information about those revolvers.

After Elias returned from his trip to Moscow, he told me casually (when he said something casually it was always very important), "Well, you certainly did not want to kill Stalin with those revolvers." Somehow the revolvers were about to disappear from the accusation. And, indeed, when I saw my file many years later, there was no sign of the revolvers.

Only years later did I find out what had actually happened. The revolvers were there, only they were not mine! They were Mr. Gyula Hevesi's, the old Hungarian revolutionary in whose maid's room I stored my things! One was an old army pistol, a souvenir, and the other a small Mauser pistol for which he did not have a permit. Apparently, he carried it whenever he had to go to faraway places in Russia. Of course, he acknowledged that they were his.

Unlike many Hungarian revolutionaries, he was not shot, but returned to Hungary, where he was in charge of scientific technical inventions. He had a very high position there, so he had a beautiful villa outside Budapest. (I am jumping ahead to when I saw him in the 1960s, in Hungary.) The villa had a glass cupola and a sunken living room. It was just unbelievably elegant, and there I met Mr. Hevesi again. Tea was brought in, with chestnut puree, heavy cream, and little petit-fours, all on the finest china. Here we apologized to each other. "I am terribly sorry to have caused you all this trouble with the guns," I said. "Oh my dear, don't mention it," he said reassuringly, "because out of the nine years I was in the NKVD prison, the revolvers only accounted for two." So there we were, very politely apologizing to each other over this lovely tea, saying, "Don't mention it, don't mention it."

I don't know what else Elias did in Moscow, but I do know that he traveled to Moscow to explore those revolvers as well as the other accusation—that I had hired my modelmaker because he was such a splendid shot. Actually, the modelmaker was recommended to me by a modern architect named Zucker who I believe eventually came to the United States and perhaps taught at the New School. I had not known Fuhlbrügge before, so I could not have known whether or not he was a good shot. Elias did interview this Mr. Zucker, the architect, which meant he actually did get proof in my favor.

I still cannot understand why Elias went to Moscow. He had obviously been sent by his superiors—he could not have done it on his own initiative. But why did Elias go to look at these revolvers when he could have happily accepted their existence in the form of a sworn affidavit stating that the building supervisor had found them? This piece of paper would have been enough to corroborate the accusation. Why did he go to the trouble of questioning witnesses in my favor?

Elias found out that the revolvers were not mine, and that I could not have invited the modelmaker for his sharpshooting ability because I did not know him before he was in Russia. In the process, he disproved the entire, orchestrated confrontation. Even more strange: Why, when these things had been disproved, did Elias continue to spend so many hours trying to trick me into signing a false confession? Perhaps it was because the factual supports of the scenario had collapsed, so an admission of the conversations became doubly important.

Fighting The Second Accusation

After the revolvers had subsided, I decided to go back to my plan of fighting the courier deposition, because more than dead you cannot be. So, I said to Elias, "I want to complain about the investigation, and I want to talk to somebody." "But Eva Alexandrovna," he said, "you never saw anybody but me. If you want to complain about me, I will call my superior and you can complain."

"But Elias Semenovich, I have nothing against you. I do not want to complain about you, I want to complain about the fact that the investigation against me is conducted against the rules of the Cheka." "Cheka" is the original, honorable name of the NKVD. "The Cheka has great honor, and its honor does not permit illegal affairs, the way this investigation is being conducted against me."

He came to me and put his hand on my shoulder saying, "Eva Alexandrovna, please tell me, confide in me, what do you have in mind?"

"Look," I said to him, "I cannot tell you exactly, because maybe I dreamt it, but I want to ask you: If there is a second deposition against me, in addition to wanting to kill Stalin, a second accusation, will you clearly accuse me to my face of this?"

And by now he knew I knew something, because there actually was a second accusation. He became pale and said, "What do you refer to?"

"I do not know what I am referring to, but I had a dream, and I know when this dream was, and I know where this dream was, and it pertained to a second accusation." I played a game with him, and he asked me how I knew this. "It's very simple. I walked out of my cell and I went there to find out. I know who directed this investigation and I know that the accused was fed information. It was illegal, the deposition was gotten illegally."

Elias was obviously nervous. "You could not get out of your cell, you were locked in."

"Well, in that case," I said, "it must have been a dream."

This went on for quite a while, and after that meeting nothing was said about it anymore, nothing. A month or so later, Elias asked, very casually, "By the way, in that dream of yours, do you know whether there was a signature against you?" I told him that there had been no signature against me. Of course, I knew there had been a signature against me but, assuming I had said that, they could not very easily have thrown out something I knew had been signed against me. By that time I was thinking very quickly; I have never been as intelligent as I was then. You cannot imagine what this sort of thing does to you.

So that is how Stalin lost his courier. That is how the whole thing disappeared. All I know from the other side is in Orlov's book, and you can read it.

There was a strange thing. Shortly afterward, they asked me if Bykhovskii knew another woman. When I said that he had had a girlfriend, named Schneider or something, they asked, "Was she a foreigner?"

Some weeks after the "courier" meeting, Elias called me in and told me that my investigation was coming to an end; that this would be the last time he would be talking with me, and the last chance I would have to save myself.

Time was running out, he said, and soon I would stand in front of the Tribunal. "This I want you to understand absolutely. If you admit, for example, that you had conversations hostile to our government with another foreigner [Bykhovskii], you have little to lose. You are a foreigner yourself. They might expel you and send you back to your country. Or you might, at worst, get a sentence of a year or two in a camp, which will go by fast."

"But it is my duty to inform you of our procedure: We can accept that he exaggerated, but not that he invented the accusation. If you say that you not did even know that he was an enemy, and that you did not have such conversations with him, you will be accused of everything. Oh, we will not shoot you, but you will be in a prison far away, so isolated that nobody will know where you are. You will never be able to work again. You will never be able to use these hands of yours again."

I did not understand what he meant then. Only much later, when I read Svetlana Alliluyeva's book (*Twenty Letters to a Friend*, 1967), did I understand what he meant. The family—or Stalin's sister-in-law, I do not know—spent fifteen years in solitary confinement and went totally, absolutely crazy, she did not know what was what. That is what awaited me.

This is how Elias was convincing me to sign a false confession. (He also told me that my mother had been trying to see me all these months, and he could easily permit a visit.)

If you are sitting here, today, in this room, you cannot believe there could be such a law—that if you say nothing you will be accused of the whole thing. But I believed it then and I should not have, because it was not true; and Elias should not have told me it was.

But I did not know that then, so when he told me this, I said, "*Ladno* (okay)."

Then he started to write. After a while I said, "What do you *monologisieerovat*?"

"Do you have such a verb in German?" he asked, without looking up. "We do not have such a verb," and he continued to write.

"What do you write?" I asked again.

He stopped and looked at me. "Well, Bykhovskii must have told you something if you knew he was an enemy, a Trotskyite. What did he tell you?"

Since I had read this book on the history of the Party, by Kronin, I knew what Trotskyism was. So, choosing the most innocuous thing I could think of, I answered. "Well, he told me about the differences of opinion between the Trotskyites and Stalin on the agricultural questions."

"Oh," he said, and he began to write about the agricultural question. No sooner had he given me this to read than it turned out that the agricultural question had turned into the killing of so many peasants,

Stalin's guilt in this, and Bykhovskii's saying that Stalin ought to be eliminated, or something like that.

By that time, I had caught on that Elias was "dotting the i's" to a dangerous degree, so I said, "Bykhovskii did not say anything about Stalin."

Elias said, "Well, what would he have said? That Stalin was a good man? Of course, he said that he was a bad man, what else would he have said?"

We fought all night over every sentence, and finally there was very little I confessed to, except that I said I knew Bykhovskii was a counterrevolutionary. Earlier I had been asked what I thought of Bykhovskii and had replied that I thought he was 110 percent loyal to the Communist Party. Their response was that I should have been suspicious; 100 percent was fine, but 110 percent—I should have been suspicious of him!

Giving In: The False Confession

Anyway, I did confess that there were conversations from which I found out that he was a counterrevolutionary, which of course was not true.

It was getting light then. Elias was standing behind his desk. Around that time, I would usually get hungry because I had gotten ulcers and could not eat the prison food anymore. (I did not know that I had ulcers but I had this sharp feeling of hunger.) So I told him I was hungry. The guard had already come to pick me up and I was halfway to the door, the guard standing next to me. Suddenly, as we stood there, Elias said in a deep and kind of shaken voice, "Eva Alexandrovna, for what you have done this night you will be hungrier than you have ever been before. And for a longer time, much longer."

As I walked back to the cell, I realized that this was not what he had been saying all along. He usually said, "You will see your mother, you will be sent out." This was completely incongruous with what had gone before, and only then did I understand that I had done wrong.

I later realized that there was no reason for him to tell me this. You see, during that night, I had signed my initials in the margin; he had insisted that I sign every sentence. He had done his duty conscientiously all through these six months, getting me to sign a false confession. And all through this time he knew that the minute I signed, I would sign my life away, or at least my next years, because many people had disappeared by that time. So I had signed a confession. He had won! But at that very moment, he told me something that was completely incongruous given the situation. It occurred to me that he really had broken down out of pity; the remark that he had blurted out as I left was an expression of pity for me. When I had signed my good life away, Elias's heart broke for me. And as I went back, I knew I had done wrong and I knew that I was not myself anymore.

Suicide Attempt

The formulation by which I decided to commit suicide was that having lost my identity, my dignity, I was no longer "I." With my dignity intact, nothing could happen to me in life or death. But now that my self-respect was lost, I was vulnerable. I composed a last poem, half-humorous, half-religious.

Back in my cell, I pulled down the piece of copper wire from the toilet tank. I wrapped a rag around it and immediately set about sharpening it by pretending to scrub the concrete floor. With the sharpened wire, I started to cut my wrist where I thought my vein was. In order not to get blood poisoning before I killed myself, I sterilized the thing with a match because, after all, it was so dirty from the floor where I had sharpened it. During the day, it did not go very deep. But that night it went deeper and deeper. I put my clothes under the bed to absorb the blood so it would not immediately go all over the floor, and hung my blanket over the side of the bed. With the wire I cut through fiber after fiber, little white nerve after little white nerve, deeper and deeper. The little white thing on the vein was very painful, this was a nerve. The tendons were very painful, but you had other worries besides the pain. I was told later that I was cutting in the wrong direction. You should cut parallel to your arm if you really want to kill yourself, and I was cutting crosswise. But it went pretty deep, and was not a clean cut; there was a mess of flesh there.

It was towards three in the morning when I was discovered. The woman guard was furious. She called the korpusnoi, and then I think the director of the whole prison came, and said, "What do you have against me?" It was a terribly black mark against him. Imagine a foreigner killing herself in his prison! "I have nothing against you," I reassured him.[11][11] He called the doctor who removed the heavy thread that I had placed into the wound for practical reasons. (I thought that if I had gone that far, it would be best to have a type of zipper, which could always get me that far again without too much work, should I decide the next time on taking my life.)

The next day was the day of rest in the prison. Nevertheless, I was called out to see two superiors of Elias Semionovich, a major and another officer. They asked me why I had tried to commit suicide. "Because Elias told me if I would not admit to a certain degree then I would be accused of the whole thing." I said it exactly as it was, and that it was a false confession. And all this was written down. Both the fake confession and the retraction became part of my file.

I had to open the bandage in front of the major so that he could judge whether the suicide attempt had been in earnest, and indeed it was very earnest. He had me take the bandage off right there in the questioning room, to look at it.

I saw Elias once more a few days later. He looked pale. "You should not have done this to me" he said, looking at the floor. "I was always good to you. I went to Moscow and made the revolvers disappear. Why did you do this to me?"

At that point, I still did not understand what I had done to him.

The investigator I saw after Elias was gone was a rather colorless person. I would be called out for questioning every few weeks. Months later, I was still there. At the end of December 1936, Shpigel, the

---

[11] "Typical of Soviet prisons was a practice ironically referred to by prisoners as Stalin's 'care for the living person.' Every possible precaution was taken to prevent people from committing suicide. Nets were stretched across the well of every staircase to prevent prisoners from throwing themselves over the banisters. Prisoners were shaved with clippers. Hunger strikes by individuals or groups were greatly feared by the prison administrations, and everything was done to break or prevent them... To people unacquainted with Soviet conditions—particularly to those familiar with conditions in fascist prisons—it seemed inexplicable that a regime which in other respects seemed to attach so little value to individual life should make such strenuous efforts to prevent suicide. The explanation was that, while the Soviet State regarded as permissible any interference with life by the appropriate organs of the NKVD, such as the departments of interrogation and justice, and shrank from nothing in carrying out its aims, the prison administration was held strictly responsible for the life of every prisoner." F. Beck and W. Godin, Russian Purge..., trans. Eric Mosbacher and David Porter (New York: The Viking Press, 1951), pp. 60-61.

Assistant Public Prosecutor came and asked me about the last interrogation with Elias: "What happened? What did Elias tell you?"

I did not realize quite yet that this was an accusation against Elias; that the Public Prosecutor's office had taken it as an accusation, and that Elias was already in prison. He had had no right to tell me that I would be accused of it all if I denied the entire accusation. And it would have never come out had I not cut myself. Only a year later, when I was sent out of the country, did I understand what had happened to Elias. On my way out I told the lieutenant who accompanied me to the border that I had never seen Elias again, and asked what had happened to him. There was no difficulty understanding because he said, "Oh, well, didn't you know?" or something like that. By that time, it was not difficult to communicate without words. From the abrupt and questioning way he looked up at me, I understood that Elias was in prison. Many of the investigators ended up in prison. He certainly did. And I certainly got him there.[12][12]

Afterwards, looking back, it is really clear that his slip of pity saved me and ruined him. Yes. And not for the record, but for you and me, I was twenty-nine years old, at the height of my intellectual capacity. Later on, one of the highest up told me, "You must have noticed everybody here liked you very much." I certainly did not notice; I thought they wanted to kill me. But spend six months with me at twenty-nine, if you are twenty-six, I mean, surely by that time Elias must have been quite fond of me, and yet he knew what was going to happen to me. I did not, but he knew, and up to that last moment he fought me for every comma—I mean he fought against me for every comma. Like Ally Adler's sister, Valentina, [Alfred Adler's eldest daughter] I would have never come out; many never came out. Many, many people died in the camps. It would have been the end of my life. He saved me by his last sentence, without planning it. It was completely genuine. There is no other explanation. He just stood there, and his voice broke when he said it. There were many conflicts and contrasts in this whole story.
in Leningrad, so we assume he survived.

---

[12] Elias' name does not appear on the lists of those executed in Leningrad, so we assume he survived.

Experiences And Memories

For a short time during the winter of 1937, my efforts at keeping sane must have faltered. The thoughts in my mind went around and around and I got very upset thinking back on my life in Russia. I asked for pen and ink to defend myself against possible reproaches, possible accusations that I had never even been accused of. There had been so many points of danger that I felt the irrational need to defend myself against these non-existent accusations.

Confusion

The reason I think this took place in winter is because that is when my mother was trying to help me by talking to the Chief Procurator in Leningrad. He said to her, "Now she's gotten herself mixed up and we have to disentangle it." The words he used were "sama soboi zaputelsia." This must have referred to my pages and pages of rambling. But they seem not to have mattered, because none ended up in my file.

I had suddenly remembered that soon after arriving in Russia, while visiting the border areas between Russia and Poland, I was told by the engineer who accompanied me that every word I said was reported back to state security agents in Kharkov. At that time I had not given any thought to this, but now it alarmed me. So I started to describe my trips to that critical area, saying that I had nothing to do with any objectionable activities there. I do not remember what I wrote, but I am sure it was terribly long. In spite of the great energy expended to keep my thoughts under control, many thoughts of things kept going around in my head, often in loops and curves that were beyond my powers of direction.

I remember that all sorts of things came into my mind, for instance my stay near the Ukrainian border which was really a defense line of the first order. And for some reason or other, I tried to explain why I had been there or who had brought me there, things completely unconnected with anything I was accused of, showing how loyal I was. I don't know what filled up these miles of densely written little defenses, but I am sure my mind was not well anymore. I got very mixed up. I wrote of assumed and presumed accusations, and ways to defend myself, as well as my past. It was a painful mixture in my head, weaving thoughts and directions and knotting them together in many ways. I accumulated huge quantities of this written material.

Berlin And Kharkov

I had gone to Russia practically on the spur of the moment. It took me less than a week to make up my mind. Before I came, my life in Berlin had been running in an even, happy sort of flow. After almost three years of a lonely life in a small town in the Black Forest, as a designer in the Schramberger Majolika Fabrik, I had come to Berlin where my mother had rented a lovely studio (Emil Nolde's old studio) for my brother Michael and me. It was on Tauentzienstrasse, just a few houses away from the Romanische Café, considered by many left or progressive intellectuals as the center of the world. It was possibly the most amusing place in Europe at the time.

Our studio was a large, two-story space which looked out on a backyard of trees. Inside were two cantilevered balconies, with cozy areas under them. From there I designed chinaware for several factories that belonged to the pottery concern, Carstens. I managed to get my boss to send a modelmaker to me, for whom I took a small apartment downstairs, which I furnished as a model shop. So the modelmaker came upstairs for the designs, and made plaster models which were then sent to the factories.

After a while, I visited these factories, deciding on the glazes or decorations, and then went on to the Leipzig Fair to help display the ware. This was quite a nice break from my work at the studio, which often consisted purely of giving the modelmaker a little sketch on a paper napkin through a slit in the entrance door.

I was living a most active social life. Several times we gave parties for a hundred people or more, studded with writers, actors, even Nobel Prize winners. Long afterwards I met interesting people who told me they had been my guests at the studio. I do not know how we collected all these people, but there were various nuclei of friends and relatives who brought their own friends. My uncle, Michael Polanyi, brought his scientist friends, including the young Leo Szilard. My childhood friend, Arthur Koestler, and my cousin, Anna Seghers, brought the writers [Ernst] Kantorowitz and Manes Sperber. My legendary grandmother, who was living a bachelor's life in Berlin, brought all sorts of sparkling wits. Among my guests were Alex Weissberg and Hans Zeisel, each of whom I would eventually marry. At these parties I may have appeared more sophisticated than I actually was.

From this well-ordered work schedule and cheerful life among these colorful people, I suddenly decided to go and see the most interesting, gigantic experiment of my time. To go to the Soviet Union at that time was an adventure. The great influx of foreign experts had not yet begun. It was a country where a revolution had taken place and although its scars had not yet healed, the Soviet Union seemed to be in the spring of its hopeful, almost utopian elatedness. It was like visiting Israel at some point in its early existence—a new country built on idealism.

From the time I was born, the concern of my family had always been social reform and the theories of Marx. During my last year at the Schramberg factory in the Black Forest, Germany was extremely politicized. It was the Weimar Republic, and the Communists and the Socialists fought each other, mostly with words, but in our factory town, with fists. The young Socialists objected to the politics of the old Socialist leaders. Everybody belonged to a party: Socialist, Communist, the Catholic Center, the Deutschnationale Volkspartei and, eventually, the Nazis.

Although I was not a participant in any political activity I was, of course, a member of the union because of my work at the factory. I was also a member of the Social Democratic party, which did not mean too much to me, but it was what most of my friends in Vienna expected me to do. During my years in Schramberg, I joined in the way of life of my landlord and landlady, miners from the Rhineland. They were a very respectable proletarian family of union organizers, and I went with them to the weekly gatherings at the union hall. With the factory workers, I went to build a little house in the forest, a few hours away, which was supposed to be their clubhouse. I watched the Nazi movement grow out of the disagreement between the two factions of the labor movement.

At the same time I was the pet of my boss, who considered it my duty (of course my pleasurable duty) to be something of a companion to his wife. They invited me to elegant hotels where they spent weekends. So, although I belonged to these two extremes in a small town, I definitely did not belong to the group of people to whom I should have belonged—namely to the white-collar workers, who at that time were to me extremely disgusting in their way of life, and no doubt future Nazis.

The news of the world always broke in on me as glimpses of history. I did not participate in political activities, like my childhood girl friend, for instance, who went to fight in the Ruhr land when there was a cause to be embraced, or later to Spain to fight for freedom. This was not my way of participating in the world. I was, I think, mostly curious. It was my curiosity that brought me into contact with my original master potter in Budapest. It was curiosity which brought me to my first job as a journeyman potter in the slums of Hamburg, and then into the working-class way of life in the Black Forest.

Now, in Berlin, I listened to a great amount of theoretical discussion concerning politics and the labor movement. Everybody around me was very much involved in the rights and wrongs of daily politics. And it was my charming, gifted cousin, Anna Seghers, who one day with her squinting eyes and lovely smile, took my Social Democratic membership card and tore it into small pieces, as she herself and her husband were good Communists.

A visa to Russia was very difficult to get. Tourism had not yet started, and unless you were invited as a foreign expert, you could not just apply for one. The only way I could go there on the spur of the moment was as my friend, Alex Weissberg's, future wife, as he had already been living there for several months working as a physicist. Alex was very pleased with this prospect, although we were not particularly in love, and it was not a very important aspect of the trip. So on January 1, 1932, I left my secure position and my beautiful studio in Berlin.

I only intended to spend a lengthy vacation in Russia—to have a good look around. And I said so to my boss. I remember, however, that later, in Russia, I got frantic letters from him: "How about the designs for the butter dish? You promised the butter dish!" I did send him the drawings for butter dishes and other items for the next Leipzig Fair.

Three of us traveled together by train from Berlin to the Russian border—Alex, myself and a slim young man who for some reason was leaving Vienna to settle in Russia. We arrived at the Russian border at night, and had to change trains because of the different width of the tracks. When we boarded the Russian train, I knew that I had come to a different world—different smells, different poverty, different luxuries: everything was different. And ever since, when I'm told that Russians do not behave as Western intellectuals expect them to, I think of that trip, when I suddenly found myself in a dark, mysterious and strange world, which I had never known before.

Now the three of us walked through the third class cars, with three wooden benches, one above the other, on either side of each compartment. If you ever saw Night Asylum, by Gorky [the stage version], it was nothing compared to what I saw then. Peasants dressed in rag or felt boots, with big coats, sitting and lying on these hard benches, filling the space up to the top, smelling, talking, looking like a theater performance—a strange, wild, weird theater performance.

I am sure we traveled first class and only walked through these strange compartments to get to the dining car. But the smell of these cars haunted me all through the years of my stay there, and even now when I think back with pity on my Russia, which was a part of my life, this smell of wet, old, poor material, of poor old stuff on the backs of people, still lingers. And each time I hear about their hardships or their difficulties in agriculture, I remember this smell with deep pity.

One day I remember coming out of the railroad station in Moscow and an old peasant woman taking hold of my coat and lifting it open, saying, "How do you manage to be such a clean little one?" To be a clean little one was practically impossible in their poverty, surrounded by this typical smell.

During our train trip into Russia, we met a small person with an aura of holiness about her. She was neat and clean and petite. She was a Polish revolutionary with fiery dark eyes and a smile of great peace. She seemed to be a sort of virgin, devoting her life to the good of others. She had no name, no occupation, no home. She was a professional Polish revolutionary. Some time later she appeared at our house in Kharkov. She was still lit from inside by a fire of conviction and self-sacrifice. When I visited Joan of Arc's home a few years ago I thought that Joan must have been like this little person.

Soon after we arrived, Alex took me to the weekly market, where you could still buy lovely hand-loomed aprons and other parts of the local costume. In the huge expanse of the market, where they sold little bits of this and that, were hundreds of men and women wrapped up to their teeth who were part of the landscape, making merry and being drunk. Again the smell of poverty and rather desperate misery.

Inside the train station (I think the market was near the train station), many men were lying on the floor with their feet wrapped, covered with sheepskin coats. Others stood patiently, leaning against the wall. I do not know if there was a loudspeaker, but somehow I understood that one of these peasants who was leaning against a wall found out that his train was leaving not when he expected, but some twenty hours later. So he went back to the same spot at the wall, leaning against it in the same position as before. It seemed to me that time was timeless here, and that the patience of the Russian peasant was as alarming as his poverty. It did not take long for me to understand that this was already a time of great emergency, of real famine in this part of the world. But it took several days before I understood what hunger was.

Alex had a neat apartment in a modern building block of two stories, attached to the Ukrainian Physical Technical Institute where he worked. I think it consisted of three rooms and a kitchen. The food situation for somebody like Alex, who had been invited as a foreign expert, was quite good. That meant that he had the right to shop in the stores established for foreigners.

Almost immediately after my arrival, I started to work at the China and Glass Trust of the Ukraine. I do not remember how I procured this job, but I was settled in an office in the Gosprom, a fortress-like, modern building, a symbol of progress, industrialization, and probably the Five-Year Plan. It was a forbidding place. The outside was of water-drenched concrete. Inside there were offices, like all offices, with lots of people. The most remarkable thing was that these people were very new to town life, which meant just one step away from peasants. This you could see in the toilets, which were western toilets, but which were obviously used by squatting on the edges of the porcelain bowls and discarding the used toilet paper in baskets nearby. The users did not want to soil these beautiful sanitary-looking objects by throwing dirty paper into them.

The head of the central administration of our industry was Comrade Vyazelskii, a wise, kind, and excellent person. Almost immediately upon my arrival, Mr. Vyazelskii put me in the charge of an engineer named Chokolov, the son a factory owner who had stayed on in order to run his father's factory for the Communists. He had studied in Heidelberg and his beautiful wife was a granddaughter of Lermontov.[13] They were rather aristocratic people. He was tall and quiet, well mannered, and

---

[13] Mikhail Yuryevich Lermontov (1814-1841), Russian Romantic writer, poet ,and painter on a par with Pushkin.

spoke English and German fluently. So it was quite natural that he was put in charge of me. (See a selection of Eva's designs done while in the USSR.)

The first thing Vyazelskii asked him to do was to take me out to the plate factory in Budyansk. This was a huge factory producing only plates, because in this country of over 200 million people, plates were the most important object which the change in agriculture and the change in the structure of the economy demanded. Up to that time, peasant families ate from one large bowl in the center of the table. But now there was collectivization, and people were supposed to eat in long rows in communal kitchens and communal dining rooms, and each person was supposed to have a plate. Well, that created the need for about 180 million plates! And the Budyansk factory, a few hours from Kharkov, produced nothing but plates in long, long tunnel kilns.

It was still early in the morning when we arrived there. We visited the director, who sat behind his desk while Engineer Chokolov and I sat facing him. The door opened, and someone brought him a small package, nicely and neatly wrapped in clean newspaper. As he unpacked it, we saw that it was a piece of light gray, fragrant sort of bread, with a very hard and crisp, beautiful crust. He broke off a piece and handed it to me. Then he broke another piece and handed it to the engineer, saying, "Take it, please!" with a most gracious and hospitable gesture. I, who just a week earlier had been in my Berlin studio among my elegant and intellectual friends, did not understand what he meant by this gesture until I realized that he was giving us a great present— part of his valuable cherished daily bread. It was the first time I understood what hunger was and what daily bread was. And, of course, I accepted it gratefully.

Later in the day, we happened to be in the dining area of the factory, where some people were sitting at small wooden tables. They were the same kind of anonymous, unhappy, poor peasants we had seen before on the train and in the market. Some were eating, leaning over an aluminum bowl with a grey mush in it, which I later found out was overcooked buckwheat kasha. Around each of these people stood a number of others of the same type, waiting, and watching to see if anything was left in the bowls. I understood later that only a certain number of meal tickets was given out each day—about two thirds of the workers had none, and were waiting to lick out the bowls of those who had already eaten. Somehow, I remember the stillness of the place. The stillness of those who were eating and the concentrated eagle stillness of those who waited to pounce upon the almost empty bowls.

Two weeks later, back in my office in Kharkov, I received on my desk a huge folder entitled "Standardization of the Sanitary Porcelain and the Household Porcelain of the Ukrainian China Trust." I did not understand a single word of it and I did not know what to do with it. Looking around, I did what everybody else did—namely sharpen pencils. After two weeks of sharpening pencils and looking around, I thought that this was too much, and I complained about my uselessness to the very wise head of the Trust, Comrade Viazelskii. He told me not to worry. "We are not a company like you are used to, but a rich, big country. We will use you well when the time comes, and we can afford to pay you meanwhile. Be patient."

But soon thereafter he sent me off again with the engineer to visit several china factories in the border areas. (It was these visits that alarmed me later, in prison, because it was here that I was told my conversations were being reported to the NKVD. I do not think I said anything suspicious, but somehow, in prison, like a nightmare, my visits to this area intruded upon my consciousness, and I felt I had to tell someone that I had in no way made any wrong use of my stay in this critical border area.)

Later in the winter of 1932, Engineer Chokolov and I took a train to another town, I believe it was called Polonnoe. But instead of arriving sometime around noon, according to the timetable, we arrived at midnight. A troika was waiting for us, like you see in the old Russian paintings. We got huge sheepskin coats which covered us entirely, with just our noses sticking out and our eyes looking out. And off we went for many kilometers, at a gallop, towards a factory in the village of Takarovka. The landscape was completely covered with snow. And out into this endless snow landscape, in the middle of the night, we rode. After a while we heard the proverbial wolves howling in the distance.

I wondered what I was doing there, instead of being in my cozy studio in Berlin. But there I was, on my way to Takarovka to visit a factory that produced electrical fixtures. An engineer there, a nice young man, who made friends with me, who talked to me, asked me to visit him in his apartment or room, which I did. He spoke Yiddish because everybody there spoke Yiddish. I do not know what he asked me or what he told me, but we had quite a long conversation.

From there, Engineer Chokolov and I went on to Baranovka. I think he left me there and went back to Kharkov. There was a huge chinaware factory in Baranovka, run by several very young, very lovely people. They seemed to me to be teenagers, young Jews. The technical director might have been twenty-one or twenty-two, and had a young wife. The union head was also quite a young woman. The Red director, too. Altogether, they were a bunch of very earnest young people. I remember the menu of the dinner they invited me to, which was fried sausage slices and buckwheat. They gave me a room which I think was in the guesthouse. It consisted of a bed in an empty little space, which was heated from the outside by an oven—that meant one wall was very hot. But they had forgotten to do what every decent housewife does, namely to paper all the little cracks around the window, leaving just a little six by eight inch window that can be opened, the rest being carefully taped shut. Well, my window was not taped shut. So I was sitting on my cot at night with my back against the one warm wall, shivering in the front, while little rats tried to jump up on the bed. Meanwhile, my candle got shorter and shorter. Whether the second night was better I do not remember. But I certainly visited the factory and talked to the artists. They made large quantities of quite nice, thin china.

The town itself was a typical shtetl. At that time, I had not even heard of the Jewish shtetls, but I knew that we were close to the area of Berdychev and other places known as Jewish centers. Later, when I read Sholem Aleichem, I recognized the little town that I had seen.

Visit to a kolkhoz

It was a sad little place; there were more hunchbacks and cripples than in other places. I remember driving through this little town in my troika with my big fur coat and taking photographs, which I think was highly improper from many points of view—probably from the point of view of making myself suspicious as well as being tactless. I later found out that this town was in the exact direction of a huge, heavy radial highway leading to the Polish border, a few kilometers away. I realized for the first time the mistake I had made by behaving like a tourist.

Soon after my arrival at this factory, the young people of the administration gathered to talk to me. I think it was the union organizer—a young woman, who told me that by now the workers were already very restless. I said, "My God, why are they so restless?" Apparently, they expected me to talk to them—to give them an opportunity to question me and to hear about how people lived beyond the border. I understood that I was the first foreigner to come to those parts since the Revolution and the war, at least fifteen years ago.

I had never before talked to a group of people publicly and was rather scared. What could I say? But knowing that they were interested in finding out about people in other china factories (I certainly was well enough acquainted with the social legislation of the German workers—how much vacation they got, what the apprenticeship was like, etc., etc.), I felt more confident. That evening I was led to a long table in a huge, dark loft building, which was already filled with thousands of dark figures. Only my table was lit. It was covered by a green cloth. I understood later that this meant I was not a party member; otherwise, it would have been a red cloth. Behind me, in a red glass, like in front of an icon, hung a little light in front of a portrait of Lenin. At my long table sat all sorts of people—I suppose the leaders of the party and the union and whoever was honored by being invited to sit at the guest of honor's table.

I was very comfortable because I knew that these people did not know German. And if I spoke in German, I could say what I wanted without being too flustered. So I started to tell them how people lived in a German factory, what their social legislation was, and if they were unionized or not—and so on and so on. At the end I found out that my audience had been drinking in every word I said with great attention because, knowing Yiddish, they understood German.

Then there was a question and answer session, and hundreds of little folded papers came my way. For a long time I kept them, because they were the most human and lovely expressions of interest. The artists, of course, asked me how the artists lived and worked in china factories. It must be understood, since my readers do not work in china factories, that china factories are the most international of organisms. The modelmakers, whether they speak Hindu, French, or Russian, have the same pride, the same self-confidence, the same brittle possibility of being offended, the same working methods, everywhere. And so have the jigger men, the casters, the mold makers, and the people who fire the kiln. They speak one international language. And china factories around the world, from Ohio to India to Japan, whether they are neat and orderly, or sloppy, all smell alike.

I was not expected to do any work or designing at this factory. It was strictly a visit to acquaint me with the factories belonging to our Trust. Since Chokolov had left, I was given into the charge of another engineer who was to accompany me home to Kharkov. On the way, I spent the night with his relatives in Kiev. The family consisted of a young couple and an old couple, living together in two rooms. I wondered where I was going to sleep. This secret was soon revealed to me: the younger woman, who was about to give birth, pushed a large movie advertisement, a billboard, between the bed and the couch, to separate me from them. The advertisement showed a movie which the young man had directed. He worked in the Kiev film industry.

I was still there at midday the next day, and they invited me to lunch. I was supposed to eat by myself, as they themselves had already eaten. So they served me a very nice meal of pozharski cutlets with whatever goes with it. They all looked on, pleased that I was enjoying myself. Only after I left did I understand that the family had no lunch or dinner that day, and that I had eaten up their complete payok, their allotted meat ration, for one full week.

When I arrived home from this first big excursion into the countryside, I found myself with a high fever and many lice, which I had obviously acquired from the huge sheepskin coat that had protected me from the cold in the troika.

I returned to these towns several more times. I was there late in 1933, and again in 1934. I was given the task of redesigning electrical fixtures, reducing the amount of metals in them, and I think that we worked quite successfully in this large factory. At some point, I stayed there with my modelmaker, Fuhlbrügge. It must have been in the spring, and we took horses and rode out into the countryside, and sometimes swam in the river. As we rode over the steppes, we often saw pillboxes camouflaged in the low hills. And sometimes it sounded hollow under our horses' hooves, and we would meet some peasant who would stamp the ground and say: "Aerodromy!" We also saw the very well built road being constructed with a great deal of sub-structure, going to what seemed like nowhere, but mainly towards the border, quite clearly preparing for heavy tanks and other such vehicles. Actually, what later was called the "battle of the bulge" in the Ukraine was fought here, or nearby. [Battle of Kursk, spring 1943.]

I believe now and I believed then that possibly I and my modelmaker were the only foreigners permitted in that area. And when I was later imprisoned, it was not so foolish of me to feel that there was something to explain or something that might have been thought suspect in our stay there.

I happened to be in Takarovka just before the exceptional harvest of 1933. The wheat stood man-high as far as the eye could see to the horizon. I drove through these wheat fields with the party boss, and he looked at them and said, "Well, after this no one will want to die." Up to this harvest there had been famine in the area. Later, when we again drove through the landscape of wheat fields after a rain, a luminous triple rainbow spanned the endless sky. Nowhere, it seemed to me, was the dome of the sky so wide as in the Ukraine. Much later, I read in The Listener that because no foreigners were permitted in this area, no one knew at the time that there had been a famine.

Famine looks terrible. Six-month old babies look like premature births, like spiders. People stand quietly, children stand about with huge tummies, water running down their legs. There was one day when my modelmaker received (like many of the top workers did) a pair of straw slippers. A peasant woman, with a broom, a charwoman, stood all day, staring at him with unending hatred. It was such an irritating and mysterious glance that it made you almost understand what witchcraft was all about.

During these days at the factory, one of the old Russian modelmakers told me that when he was young, and times were good, he got the following meal: old bread soaked in water, with a few drops of sunflower oil. This constituted a good meal when he was young. But today, he said, the young people did not know how to live. He knew how to live: when he got a small glass of barley, half of the barley he cooked, the other half he halved again. Then he exchanged the quarter glass of barley for a glass of milk, and for the other quarter, he bought a few drops of sunflower oil. He cooked the quarter glass of barley, poured the milk on it, and still had a few drops of oil, which was plenty for the day. He did not see why young people nowadays did not know how to manage as well as he did.

Most of the workers at the factory were starving. There was no hiding the fact. Around us in the peasant villages people had eaten up their cows, horses, cats and dogs, and it was rumored that they were now eating each other. The wheat was getting ripe, but the people were literally too weak to harvest it. So from the towns came hundreds of students to help. Two young women doctors also went out to help with the harvest. They had become my friends. The wheat was cooked in the fields to feed the harvesters, but as it was still green, most of them got terrible cramps, including my two doctor friends, but particularly the starving people.

The next year, unbelievably, everything seemed forgotten. They had not yet raised any cattle, but they had raised chickens which are very quick to grow, and they had bread. It seemed as if they had forgotten those who had starved.

It was not easy to travel to and from the Takarovka factory. I remember twice arriving there by truck. In 1934, I came back from visiting my mother (who had been very sick in Vienna) via Shepetovka. I stopped in Polonnoe to try to reach the factory, which was just a day's ride away. That was the distance we had gone by the troika the first time I went there. It was fall, and I had high leather boots, a leather coat and a leather sort of pilot's cap. I was well protected. I carried a heavy suitcase. When I phoned the factory they said, "Go to this and this crossing and wait for a truck." Well, I went to the crossing. It was raining, and at the crossing the mud was about two feet deep. I somehow managed to wait until night fell. By that time I was very cold and hungry, and I managed to stay overnight in something called the Red Cross Shelter. It was an empty, cold little house and I slept on the floor. At dawn, I continued my wait for the truck. I think it was noon when another truck passed me, a truck from a different china factory. They found me with tears streaming down my face, standing in the mud at this crossing. They said, "For heaven's sake, what are you doing here?" and took me into a factory office, warmed me, poured tea into me, fed me and phoned so that the truck to Takarovka would pick me up there. Well, I finally was sitting on this truck headed for Takarovka, with all the other travelers who were going in that direction. Suddenly the truck got stuck in what seemed to be a lake. But it was only a deeper area of mud. (It was the same mud that would defeat the German Army.) We all got out and started to push. Eventually we found ourselves at the other edge of this mud lake. It was midnight by the time I arrived at Takarovka, and everyone was asleep. I was furious, so I made a great deal of noise, waking up the director who responded by shouting: "What a time to arrive!" That was one of my approaches.[14][14]

Another time I came on a truck, and I remember a very beautiful sight. On this truck sat a rabbi, with his wife—like a Rembrandt painting, perfectly still—unbelievably clean, neat, at peace and very dignified. He with a long white beard, she with a kerchief on her head, sitting very close together, motionless through the whole trip. On a different trip, my train was delayed until the next day, so I slept on the long, wooden table in the train station. I awoke to find many people having breakfast around me, not wanting to disturb my sleep.

In prison I wrote about all these memories for days, and everything was given to the Chief Prosecutor of Leningrad. The writings were tangled skeins of thoughts and must have been impossible for him to decipher; even I had difficulty unraveling these memories in the long months that followed.

Called out again

Once during these next months I was called out by a very high-up man. I did not understand why. I had not seen him before, and it seemed strange. He said, "You know the way we function. If there are two people in the room and one says you had some hostile or counterrevolutionary conversations, if there is no third witness, we believe the accuser, and you have to prove that you did not say this. That is our rule." "Well, in that case," I said, (and I always remember these words in Russian: В этом случае судебная практика является жалким ремесла) "in that case, jurisprudence is a pitiful craft." This took place after the confrontation and the whole story, so I said, "Why don't you call Bykhovskii, and then you will see who says the truth." At which point he leaned forward and said slowly, in French, "Impossible," which gave me the creeps. Evidently, Bykhovskii was already dead.

I could not figure out why he had called me in. Later on, I thought that this might have been the time when the head of the Leningrad NKVD was secretly watching me through a peephole, or a one-way

---

[14] On another trip, Eva had to spend the night in a train station. Rather than sleeping on the floor, she slept on a long table, in her leather boots and coat. She awoke to find other travelers having tea around her. They hadn't wanted to disturb her by waking her up.

mirror. It was quite clear that he had seen me, because when I met him six months later for what I thought was the first time, he remarked about my having lost so much weight.

Hope

Shortly after this strange meeting, I was called into the office again and told that I would soon be sent out of the country. I was even asked which way I wanted to be sent. I was flabbergasted. I had been waiting to be shot. Now they were asking me about my travel preferences. It took a little while for me to adjust, but I decided that I should say I wanted to go to London, to my uncle [Michael Polanyi]. I could not very well choose to be sent to Germany, from where I had come. Then I went back to my cell and started to wash my slippers, the slippers of red leather with the big, beautiful, long goat's hair all over. I started to prepare, and I washed the goat's hair of my slippers perfectly white, snow white.

Faked Evidence

The next day I was called out again by the same investigator, this time to a different room. I heard a click and again thought we were being listened in on. "We have now found new evidence against you," he said, "and we are going to accuse you of the whole accusation and put you in front of a Military Tribunal." This meeting took place in early May 1937, one year after my arrest. He showed me a photograph I had taken seven years earlier of a pistol with a clearly legible serial number. This was the photograph they confiscated when they arrested me. (I still have the photo in my attic.) He told me that they had found this very same pistol, the one in the picture, with the same serial number!

I protested. "This gun belonged to somebody I stayed with in Germany, many years ago." (The photograph had come from Mr. Leichsenring's house, in Schramberg. He was a representative of the insurance company of the German unions, and I had lived with his family for a while.) I had taken this photograph in 1929. Now it was 1937, so they could not have gotten this gun.

"It is not possible!" I told him. I did not say exactly that, but I said "anything can be fabricated and certainly a number like this," and got up. From the window, I could see a huge courtyard of cellblocks. I made a big gesture with my arm, and said, "With this power you can prove anything, and I am totally powerless to prove otherwise. If you say there is a submarine under my bed, I am not able to prove there is no submarine under my bed."

But he insisted that they had new evidence; whether this picture would have been the new evidence I don't know, but there is no question that that gun, with that number, would have been a complete fake. Then I was taken back to my cell. I had washed my slippers out, permitting myself to dream about freedom, the sea voyage; I dreamt so much that for the next five and one-half months I had to push those two days of dreaming out of my memory. They were too painful to remember, those two days of dreaming, of indulging in the vision of the sea and in my vision of freedom.

Waiting time

That was the last human contact I had for five and one-half months, except for the guards. For the last five and one-half months of my imprisonment, they did not call me out. Nothing, nothing, nothing. They hardly took me out for walks, certainly not every third day for seven minutes. They let me stew there, getting sicker and sicker, more and more nervous.

I had been put on ice. The food had gotten much worse. It was terrible. My ulcers were getting worse too, even though by that time I was getting a glass of milk every day because the doctor had prescribed it, plus a small piece of light gray bread, also the doctor's prescription. I knew that if the door opened, either I would be handed my written accusation based on this new "evidence," and the date of my tribunal, or a miracle would happen. With such an accusation I could be shot anytime. So I waited. I got a tic in my face, and my shoulder was jumping. I was very nervous.

Expulsion

Without any notice, on September 8 [1937], the door opened and I was taken out to the same, colorless investigator. Two people were sitting near him, one left and one right. He started to shout at me: "This is your last chance to admit your guilt; this is your last chance. Now you will be going to trial. We know everything about you." And after he shouted for maybe two hours (they had lots of time to shout), he gave me a paper. It was dated April 10, 1937. This was the paper that said the highest Soviet tribunal had decided to cancel its [previous] decision, to send me out of the country.

The meaning that hit me was that they had canceled the decision to send me out of the country that they had made six and a half months before [Feb. 14, 1937]. What it actually meant was they had cancelled their decision to put me before the Military Tribunal, (meaning the death penalty) and really were going to send me out of the country. But I didn't understand that. So I waited for the next paper: the accusation. [See "Cancelling Terrorist Charges," next page.]

Instead of that, they gave me my passport, with a new picture in it, and told me to sign it. My God, I thought, what pedantic sort of people, to be shot I need a new passport. (I never knew that my old one was missing.) My old passport photo showed me holding a cigarette in front of my mouth, which hid my face enough so that anyone could have used it. I assumed they had stolen my passport, knowing I was about to be shot. So here was the new passport that I was supposed to sign, and I signed it. The two people, left and right, were obviously there to witness my signature. I noticed some extra papers in the passport and asked what they were. "We want to get you out of the country, and this is your Polish visa." I looked at it and, although I could not read Polish, it seemed from the numbers that it was only good for a short time. I think it had to be used by September 17. Again, he said, "We will send you out of the country."

By that time, I already had what my husband, Alex, called a very rested head, so I said, "Out of the country? Why? I haven't done anything wrong, I want to stay here." He was taken aback.

"After all," he countered, "there was this big accusation and we can't really take any chances nowadays."

"But I didn't do anything wrong. And anyway, I want to find out what this means? The Russian constitution permits any country to join the USSR, and I'm absolutely sure that before long many countries will desire to join the USSR. I want to know whether I am expelled from the present territory of the Soviet Union or from all future territory?"

He did not know what to say. Such chutzpah had never yet come to him, even in his dreams. He did not know the answer, and I still do not know the answer. I knew I would have to be at the border by the 17th. I was taken back to my cell and was in bed asleep by 9 pm. Early in my stay, I had been up at night a lot because they investigated you at night. But for the last five and one-half months, I had had a very regular life and more normal sleeping time.

Three hours later, at midnight, I was woken up and taken to see the head of the whole Leningrad NKVD, whom I had never seen before. I thought I looked very beautiful because I had pressed all the little pleats on my blouse with my spit, and I wore what had been a nice, blue skirt. The skirt was unfortunately full of spots, and it had gone to pieces a bit, but I still thought I was elegant. They were my own clothes, but I mean how much can you have left after sixteen months? I had put this on specially when they woke me, because I thought I might be let out.

I was taken to a very beautiful office. I really did not know the meaning of it all, but I remember that I could not stay awake and asked to wash my face. There was a little powder room there, and when I looked at myself in the mirror I looked terrible; there were huge dark circles under my eyes. When I had looked into the mirror of the toilet in my cell, I had not looked so bad, but when I looked into a real mirror I couldn't believe my eyes. (A few days later, when I was on the train going out of Russia, I asked a stranger sharing my compartment how old he thought I was. Trying to be very complimentary, he said, "You can't be a day over forty-five.") I was thirty.

Then the head of the NKVD spoke: "So many people have signed for you: Joffe, the greatest physicist—I play tennis with him. He was here in the office to guarantee for you. You must know what that means. How well do you know him?" I answered, "Not well enough to guarantee for him." I wasn't very bright late at night. He showed me some of the letters and I was surprised to see who had written on my behalf. [See Appendix D.]

Then he said, "Well, you lost some weight." And I realized it had been he who had observed me through the one-way mirror or peephole five and one-half months earlier. "I couldn't eat the food anymore," I replied. He turned to the brutal-looking blond man standing next to him: "She didn't get proper food? She didn't get...?" For the last five and a half months I should have gotten restaurant food, and apparently it was an oversight that I hadn't. I should have been getting restaurant food, because that five and one half months had been "waiting time." Anyone who is to see someone high-up in Russia must wait for many months; not only I, anyone. Jascha had to wait three months to see his superior, Slutsky. People who wanted to see the Commissar of Light Industry (the Commissar in my field), waited for weeks and weeks. Apparently this had been "waiting" time, not "punitive" time, and because of that I should have been getting proper restaurant food rather than prison fare.[15]

Then the NKVD head asked about my uncle, Michael Polanyi. "Don't you think Michael Polanyi might in some way work for us?"

"No, I don't think so."

And then he changed the subject. "What are you going to do now when you are sent out? You will certainly now go to a sanatorium for a few weeks."

Unfortunately I didn't go to a sanatorium, but they were quite clear that I should. "Well, what are you going to do?"

"I'm going to marry Hans Zeisel."

Then he asked me who else I could marry, and when I said, "Nobody," he nicely said, "Don't be silly, of course there must be many people waiting for you." They were quite complimentary that way.

At this point they mentioned Jascha again, saying he was on a "punitive mission." I did not understand exactly what they meant.

Invitation To Spy For Russia

Then, I do not know how it came up, I found out that they knew Hans belonged to a circle of Viennese Social Democrats. The NKVD head went on, saying that they were getting hostile leaflets from the Viennese Social Democrats (I am sure that this was true), and that they were now convinced that I was their friend, and they would like me to tell them if I knew of any hostile action against them. "You are such a believable person," he said, "Everybody believes you."

---

[15] "These [foreign prisoners] were given special privileges in respect to food and treatment before their expulsion." F. Beck and W. Godin, Russian Purge..., trans. Eric Mosbacher and David Porter, New York: The Viking Press, 1951, p. 62.

"Because I tell the truth. Of course I am believable. But do not think that a German officer, or anybody in the military, would believe a word. I'm not their type."

"Well," he went on, "we don't want you to do anything like that. We just want you to inform us if there is any hostile activity against us. For instance" and now, he pointed out four areas:

The first area was the Viennese Social Democrats, which he had already mentioned.

The second area they wanted to know about was the German newspaper in Budapest, the Pester Lloyd. I was surprised. "But the Pester Lloyd is a Jewish newspaper." And he replied, "Any German language newspaper is a focus, a nest, with the beginning of a Nazi influence. Any German newspaper, wherever it is, has the germ of Nazism." I knew who ran that newspaper and this seemed very improbable to me.

The third was the Klatschko family, who had been close friends of my family for several generations. This gave me the creeps because they were also close to Trotsky. They were his best friends. The Klatschkos were the people Trotsky stayed with when he was in Vienna. My childhood swings had gone to the Trotsky children through the Klatschkos.

At some point Mrs. Klatschko, the old revolutionary lady, had come to Russia while I was still working there, and I couldn't believe that she was not on a political, pro-Trotskyite mission. That was a very dangerous acquaintance for me to have had at that time. I was now very much afraid that the Russians were going to push me into a Trotsky affair of some sort, perhaps try to send me to Trotsky through the Klatschkos.

Then they asked me about the fourth area, Hans' field—market research. About two years earlier, Paul Lazarsfeld, a founder of sociology, had gone to the U.S. They knew exactly that market research had come to America. He asked me whether I did not believe that the market research survey was a cover for a spy organization. I told him that I was sure it was not, to which he said, "Why? What do you know?" "That's my instinct," I replied. "Well, from now on you must never trust your instincts. This has nothing to do with military spying, but if you know of something that is against us...." and then he told me to write to a certain address with some disappearing ink between the letters, and gave me a code name, which I promptly forgot. Then a guard accompanied me back to my cell. And as we went over a bridge, he said, "This is your last trip over the Bridge of Sighs." And so I was back in the cell. Suddenly they called me out again, and I thought, Oh my God, something terrible has happened. They called me back to tell me that they had caught a real spy, named Ladislas Farago, and let him go by accident.

Farago

The head of the NKVD wanted me to try to find Farago, and to let them know where he was. "He's probably in Prague, but since Vienna is the main center of spying nowadays, Farago could be in either place. Find him," he said. I told him I would try, and then he asked what I would say to him when I found him. "I will tell him that I got his name by knocking at the wall."

"You were knocking at the wall?" asked the NKVD man, somewhat surprised.

"Of course I was knocking at the wall."

When he found out that I had learned about knocking from an old Russian movie, he said, "A Soviet movie, and it shows how to knock? I have to go after this movie."

I never found Mr. Farago, but I did hear that he had been in Czechoslovakia. (I heard nothing of Mr. Farago for a long, long time until, when we were in Europe in 1957, our friend Leo Frischauer sent someone to rent our house in Rockland County. Who else but Mr. Farago! He turned out to be the man who wrote that book on spies.[16][16]. He was an official spy. It was terribly funny, because suddenly there he was living in our house. I don't think he paid the rent.)

Frantic Trip to the Train Station

That was the very last hour. I knew I had a passport taking me through Poland, and I knew that I couldn't wait very much longer because my Polish visa was expiring. After sixteen months of being a very good prisoner, never in any way making any fuss, I started banging at the

---

[16] *The Game of the Foxes* (London: Hodder & Stoughton, 1972).

door and shouting, "My God, My God, I'm going to miss my train." They got the big korpusnoi and I said, "I must go away." He eventually brought me two suitcases. I did not know my mother had sent any suitcases, but she had; she thought I was going to Siberia and she wanted me to have warm clothes. So there were these two heavy suitcases. Then they took me to the place where you wait when you first come into prison. There was a desk, some other people and several guards. They took out a document that said when I had arrived. "You came in May 1937," the guard read aloud. "No," I said, "May '36." People usually stayed there six months, because six months was the maximum time for an investigation. Why I stayed a year and four months I do not know, but I had been there longer than anybody else.

A lieutenant was there who was supposed to take me to the border, and he asked me what I wanted for the trip. "Toothpaste," I told him.

"Toothpaste? But you must have *pomadochku* and *pudruchku*" [lipstick and powder]. I told him that I did not need *pudruchku* and *pomadochku*, I needed toothpaste, but it did no good. He asked me what shade of *pudruchku* I used, and I told him Rachelle (a brownish pink). So I sat in this place, where there was a big clock, and I just watched the clock, knowing that the train was leaving very soon. I was extremely nervous. If there was one thing I did not want to do, it was to stay in that prison. But I sat and waited while he went off to find *Rachelle Pudruchku*. Suddenly he appeared, put his hands up and exclaimed: "I couldn't get Rachelle, I got this other color." By that time the train was about to leave. There were four other guards, I think, and they all took me and the suitcases and we ran out to a large black limousine. Either you travel in a large black limousine, like in the movies, or in a prison van. We got into the limousine, two guards with bayonets sat in front and two in back with me. When we arrived at the train station we jumped out of the limousine, my guards running with the heavy suitcases, and came to the train just as it started slowly moving. We just barely made it, and I began to laugh, because I always "just barely make the train," you see. The guards tossed up the suitcases and the four of us jumped onto the train.

Ride to the polish border

Two guards and the lieutenant were to accompany me on the two-day trip to the border. When the conductor came, he saw that the lieutenant and two guards had first class tickets and I had to go third class. It was very hard for them to convince him that they were guarding me, and therefore we had to be together. I remember that, although it was September, I had on a raccoon jacket which Mother had sent to me. I felt very elegant in it, even though it wasn't in very good condition. By the time we finally came to Minsk, where we were to spend the night, the lieutenant had taken a liking to me and said he would try to phone ahead so they would put me in a hotel instead of the prison. When we got to the station, I had to go to the ladies' room. Now the ladies' room, of course, is only for ladies. So the two male guards with the bayonets stood outside while all the women were inside. It seemed to me that there was very much commotion because I hadn't been used to any commotion at all. As I came out, he said, "I received instructions. You have to go to the prison." Then he saluted and said, "But it's a very good prison, we prepared it for ourselves." So I was taken to this very good prison, prepared especially for NKVD people. As you know, everything for NKVD people was very good, including this prison. After all, they had all the privileges.

It was an old kind of fortress, with huge walls three quarters of a yard thick, and a very narrow staircase. The walls were painted a greenish-grey, and on the stairs was a brand new, braided runner, very colorful and folkish. It was quite a contrast to the grey walls. I was searched again, which was very disagreeable—stripped naked and searched. And then I came into a rather dark, large room-like cell. Next door somebody was knocking with such speed that I knew he must have been in prison very long. When I knocked, it was much slower. His knocking sounded just like Morse code, it was so fast I couldn't follow it.

Next day I was taken out and joined on the trip from Minsk to the border by two other former prisoners. They told me there had been water up to their knees in other prisons. It was absolutely horrible in the other prisons. One of them was a German math teacher who had a red Afro because his hair had been cut everywhere the same length, and it stood out. The other was a small, lively Polish spy. The Polish spy had been in one of the camps for nine years and said proudly, "Now I will be hailed as a hero in Poland." He had been a bookkeeper and actually had not been treated terribly badly, and now he was going home to be a hero.

At the Russian/Polish border

When we finally came to the border, the three of us were taken into the office of the head of the NKVD, who sat behind a large desk. Each one of us had a guard behind him, with a bayonet. The NKVD man asked us whether we held any grudges or had any bad feelings about Russia. Everybody said they had no grudges except me. I told him that I couldn't read Polish, but that it seemed to me my visa started on the seventeenth, and that this was only the sixteenth. "I don't want to get into a Polish prison, I'm quite used to your prisons, and I would like to be kept here another day until my visa becomes valid." The NKVD man laughed: "Your neighbor is a Polish spy, and he can read Polish very well. Please read her visa." The little Polish spy read it to me, and it meant something else, which was quite different, so it was all right. We all signed, saying that we had no grudges, and then he gave us each ten dollars to spend on the other side of the border. "Whoever has any Russian money left can buy sausage or something to take along." Since I had money (Mother had sent me some to buy cigarettes) the others asked me to buy them sausage and vodka, which I did. So I bought for everybody. The head of the secret police found this whole thing very funny and said, "Well, now you can order some dinner."

At the border is a very elegant Intourist restaurant for visitors, but we sat in the NKVD office. In came a waitress with a white apron and a menu. The menu was passed from one to the other and, since I had the money, they asked me if they could have this or that, and then ordered it. They brought in a table with a white damask cloth, china, glassware and heavy silver. Then came the waitress with all these goodies. I sat at the head of the table, and behind each one of us stood a very hungry guard with his bayonet. First came a big metal tureen on a pedestal, full of borscht, with sour cream next to it. The man at the desk said, "Eva Alexandrovna, you are the little hostess, why don't you serve?" So I was the little hostess, giving everybody his borscht and smetana. We had this very elegant meal, on china, after none of us had had anything but an aluminum bowl and a wooden spoon for years.

When the train came, we were given a whole compartment to ourselves. The three of us and the three guards got in. We rode through no man's land towards a big arch. When I had first come to Russia the banner on it said, "Welcome, World Revolution." Now it had been changed to "Welcome to the Home of the Working People." The train slowed down under the arch and the guards jumped off. We were so excited that we ran back and forth in the corridor; it was the first time we were able to walk without anybody behind us.

Invitation to Spy for Poland

On the other side of the border was a telegraph bureau where I telegraphed Mother to tell her I was out. The Pole was just beside himself with joy. He said that the Red Cross would now accept him, and coddle him, and love him, and he was just so very happy to be in Poland. I don't know how happy a Pole can be, but he was certainly happy. Finally there was only the math teacher and I left on the train. We sat in a compartment, and a third man came in, who began asking us all sorts of questions. When the conductor came, he showed him a green card. This fellow had a long, triangular face and tremendously large and brutal hands. I saw his hands, and it did not make me comfortable. I don't think it took him too long to say that he was from the Polish General Staff, and that he had also been in prison in Russia for many years, as well as in a camp. Then he pointed at one of the houses and said "That's where I really live, over there." He explained that he was most interested in people coming out of Russia, particularly foreigners who came from prison, because the Poles were collecting information on Russian industry. They had a large map in Warsaw, and any information we could give him, particularly the German math teacher, would be put down on that map. Information about electrical systems in the factories would be most valuable. He said that he spoke to everyone who came out. Recently he had had a long talk with a German journalist from Die Neue Freie Presse who was traveling through Poland.

"And Litvinov," he continued, "the foreign minister, he came through here with his bags stuffed with dollars. He won't return." He did return, though. I don't know how much this man was making up. When he walked out for a minute, the math teacher whispered to me, "I won't give him anything, I'm taking all my information to Berlin." So then somehow, soon, we lost the math teacher. I hadn't talked to anyone, but to nobody, for a long time, except during these last few days. So I was in a very talkative mood. When the man from the General Staff returned I told him I had been in prison for sixteen months. "I can't believe that," he said, and to prove it I took the piece of the metal can, the kind of a "knife," out of its hiding place in my shoe. My shoes were already in very bad condition; I remember that they were brown, Bally shoes. He kept talking, saying, "You know, I go back and forth to Moscow, and nothing happens to me. When I am in Moscow I use this union card." He showed me the [green] card of a baker's union. "I'm a baker when I'm there. You can't live in Russia without a union card. It's like an I.D. card. Nothing happens to me," he went on, "because Yezhov [who was then head of the NKVD] is our man. Last week I was sitting opposite him in his office; you know, he sits crooked, like this. I know him well."

Through our conversation he found out that I had been accused of trying to kill Stalin and, after a while, he said, "You know, you could be very useful to us, and we could pay you well." He wanted to send me back there as a Polish spy, assuring me that nothing would happen because Yezhov would protect me. "What you do is go in by glider, which makes no noise at all. The peasants expect a glider, and when you come down they will lead you. We will pay you a thousand rubles."

"A thousand rubles is nothing." I told him. "I made thousands of rubles as a designer. Anyway, I wouldn't go back under any circumstances."

The conversation continued along these lines. and he told me that Vienna was then the center of all intelligence activity. "That's wonderful." I said to him. "I'll give you a very good address in Vienna." So I gave him the address of Shura, who was a very staunch Communist. She could do anything she felt like with a Polish spy, as long as she knew he was a Polish spy, whatever she wanted to. "She might be very willing to help you," I said, "but I am very tired. I will have nothing to do with it." I don't know why I gave him her address. I was so furious at him.

Incommunicado in Warsaw

When we arrived in Warsaw, the man from the General Staff took me to a hotel and asked me what I was going to do now that I was free. I told him I was going to marry a man named Hans Zeisel.[17] A few minutes

---

[17] Eva and Hans Zeisel (a young lawyer and sociologist) had known each other for years, and he had long wanted to marry her. He visited her several times in Russia, and on one of these visits they decided to marry. Hans was waiting for her in Vienna when she got out of prison.

later. when I signed the hotel register, I looked at the guest list and there was the name "Hans Zeisel," on the same page I had just signed. Of course Hans had not been there, and I have no idea what it meant.

Shortly thereafter, I found that I was incommunicado. I couldn't call Vienna. I couldn't call anybody. The desk wouldn't give me a connection. That's how this general staff person had arranged it. Here I was in this Polish hotel without anyone knowing where I was. It's quite clear that they were just as much afraid of me as I was of them. They thought maybe I was a Russian emissary, maybe even a Russian spy.

To the Polish/Czech Border

Whatever he thought, he made sure I didn't stay in Poland by giving me a "guide" from border to border. The next morning this same man picked me up, took me to the train, and put me into a compartment. There was a gentleman in the compartment already and, when the conductor came this gentleman pulled out the same kind of green card. By that time I knew that the green card belonged to the Polish General Staff. So here, sitting opposite me, was another of those people. Soon after the train started, this man got up to take a photograph out the window. The peculiar thing was that, although he was pointing the camera out the window and looking through it very intently, the lens was on the side of the camera pointing straight at me. Oh, what a joke. Anyway I must tell you that after being so much on edge, this did not please me. The whole thing did not please me, because it was very dangerous. So finally, I made it to Czechoslovakia, and was rid of him. That was the last of the Poles. When my mother arrived from Russia via Poland about three weeks later, the first Polish spy, the one with brutal hands, was expecting her. He gave her my regards and told her I had been accused of trying to kill Stalin, and that I was all right. He also gave her the spy spiel, but he didn't offer to send her back on a glider.

Riding alone on the train in Czechoslovakia, I composed a fond farewell poem to my cell number 4.

Looking back

Looking back on my five years and nine months in Russia, after almost half a century of housewifery and career, I see myself in all these peculiar situations—galloping over secret aerodromes, hearing the wolves howl at the edge of the snowy steppes, riding in a troika, standing in tears in the mud in Polonnoe, speaking in a dark hall to thousands of Yiddish workers, sixteen months in Stalin's prisons—in all these situations I see myself still as a young girl from a good family who considers herself the quintessence of normalcy. Even being shouted at by investigators, or standing in front of a Marshall of the Soviet Union, or up in the tower of Notre Dame with a Red general [Paris vacation with Jascha], or washing the floor of my cell with a rag hiding a copper wire, sharpening it to cut my veins while I produced a cheerful poem to accompany me to the other side.

In all these circumstances, I felt I did the proper thing, always using common sense and minding my manners. Through all the friendships and the passionate loves and tears, I remained a prude. I was definitely naive. My life has consisted of navigating through anecdotes that have shown me the world in so many of its aspects. It is perhaps true that I was more curious than others.

After I came out of prison, my friends who had been Communists turned sharply and zealously against the terror in Russia, which by then was at its height, and which some of them, like Alex, had experienced first-hand.[18] Many of them, long before the 1956 Hungarian Revolution, had become anti-Communists. And the anti-Communism of these intellectuals was just as wild and outspoken and full of hatred as their Communism had been before. My friends, Koestler and Alex, and even people later, in America, who knew that I had been in prison, could not understand why I had not become a wild anti-Communist. In fact I never was an anti-Communist, even in prison. I was what I called a "former non-Communist." A former non-Communist can't become a former Communist. I could not accept the sharp and bitter attitude of former Communists against their earlier ideals. Having been a tourist in the world and not a participant, not a fighter like they were, I did not become a fighter against Communism.

In fact, I have kept my sentimental love of Russia with all its tints of pity and respect, because when I first entered Russia, it hit my soul

---

[18] While Eva was still in prison, Alex was arrested and imprisoned by the NKVD. After the Molotov–Ribbentrop Pact, in 1939, they turned him over to the Gestapo, who imprisoned him again. This is described in Alex's extraordinary autobiography, *The Accused*.

deeply. And ever since, my heart has gone out to the Russian people, with their suffering, patience, poverty and naiveté, their kindness and patriotic chip on the shoulder, and particularly their vulnerable pride.

I wrote two more prison poems after my release. The first was on a visit to a man I had loved in my youth, saying how you always have a home with someone you truly loved.

The last poem I wrote six months later, when I had to flee from Vienna as Hitler's troops marched into Austria.

Appendix A: My Mother

by Jean Richards

Eva Zeisel is considered by many to be one of the leading American industrial designers of the 20th century. Her designs are in the permanent collections of major museums around the world. She has received the highest medals from the Hungarian government, an honorary doctorate from the Royal College of Arts, London and several lifetime achievement awards in the U.S., including the National Design Award.

During her long life—she lived to 105—Eva worked in many countries. One of them was Russia. When she was 28, and working in Moscow as Artistic Director of the Russian China and Glass Trust, she was arrested. Caught up in the early Stalinist purges, Eva was falsely accused of conspiring to assassinate Stalin. At one point an interrogator actually accused her of a successful attempt on Stalin's life, at which point she said, "But Stalin is still alive. How successful could it have been?" He replied, "Don't make bad jokes." Eva was considered an extremely dangerous criminal and spent the next sixteen months, mostly in solitary confinement, in cell #4 of the Leningrad prison known as Bolshoi Dom, the Big House.

● ● ●

My mother, Eva Zeisel, née Eva Amalia Striker, aka Eva Alexandrovna Stricker[19][1], was born in Budapest, in 1906, into an upper middle class, intellectual, assimilated Jewish family. As Hungary was then part of the Austro-Hungarian Empire, she had Austrian citizenship.

Eva began as a gifted painter but, at her mother's suggestion, decided to learn a craft, so as not to have to starve in a garret. At the age of nineteen she apprenticed herself to the last master potter in the medieval guild system in Budapest, learning all aspects of pottery, from mushing clay with her feet, to taking the wares to market. Six months later she graduated as a journeyman.

---

[19] The name Striker is spelled variously in the NKVD documents, and elsewhere. The German pronunciation of Striker, transliterated into Russian, was spelled Shtrikker or Shtriker. We have retained the spellings as they occur in each document.

After starting her own pottery, Eva worked first at a Hungarian factory, then in a ceramics shop in the red light district of Hamburg, and then, for two years (1928-1930) at the Schramberger Majolica Fabrik in the Black Forest of Germany. There she designed hundreds of pieces of tableware, keeping hundreds of workers busy.

From the small town of Schramberg, Eva moved to Berlin, where her mother had rented Emil Nolde's former studio for Eva and her brother Michael, a patent agent and engineer. Eva worked there for the Carstens factory and, according to her legendary grandmother, Cecile Pollacsek (known as Cecil Mama), she became "inebriated on amusements." These were the two most elegant years of Eva's life. Her studio was a sort of open house, and she sometimes gave parties for as many as 100 people, including all sorts of artists and intellectuals. Among these were physicists Leo Szilard and Victor Weisskopf, writers Arthur Koestler (a childhood friend), Manes Sperber, and Anna Seghers, as well as two future husbands, Alex Weissberg and Hans Zeisel.

Eva writes about the decadent atmosphere and art of pre-Nazi Berlin, and contrasts it with the arts that were coming from Russia: lovely children's books, choruses, cabarets, theaters and folk dances. In addition, the great Russian utopian experiment sounded intriguing, so one day, rather suddenly, she decided to "see what was behind the mountain." It was almost impossible to get a visitor's visa, so she went as the fiancée of her good friend, Alex Weissberg, whom she later married. Alex had moved to Kharkov a year earlier, to work as a physicist/engineer in a new technical institute. Eva's visit to Russia turned into five years of work and adventure, the last 16 months spent in a Stalinist prison.

Soon after arriving in Kharkov, Eva visited the Ukrainian Glass and Porcelain Trust, and was promptly hired. The director of the Trust sent her to far-off factories to familiarize herself with their capabilities and techniques. Later, the Trust assigned her to design porcelain tableware at the Lomonosov factory (formerly the Imperial Porcelain Factory) in Leningrad. This was not a good working situation, as Eva felt that the factory was not focusing on her designs. Perhaps this was because she was working there at the behest of the Trust, and her work would not be counted as part of the factory's Five Year Plan. During this period, Eva arranged for a German modelmaker, Hermann Fuhlbrügge, to come to Russia to assist her. Still, the working conditions did not improve, so she decided to leave the factory and return to Kharkov. But before leaving she participated in and helped organize an important porcelain exhibit at Central Trade Hall (*Torgovaia plata*) in Moscow.

Eva told us about two late-night visitors to this exhibition: Yagoda, head of the NKVD and Voroshilov, Minister of War. Yagoda asked why some pieces were not as white as others, and Eva's colleague explained that one needed kaolin, now in short supply, to make the clay whiter. Yagoda replied that he had plenty of "free labor" that could mine it. This gave Eva the creeps.

Around midnight, Voroshilov arrived and, at his request, Eva showed him around, giving him a lecture on aesthetics. A photo of Eva and Voroshilov, taken at this exhibition, was later confiscated from Alex Weissberg's apartment when he was arrested (1937).

The decision to participate in this exhibit was fortuitous for Eva. It was there that the director of the huge, Dulevo Porcelain Factory, impressed with her designs, offered her a job. She accepted, and for the next year she guided an experimental laboratory for mass production, designing four new tea and coffee services, a set for serving water, a liqueur service, special tableware for kindergartens, eggcups, vases and a smoker's set. Many of these were beautifully decorated by chief artist Petr Leonov, who often used traditional, Russian textiles as inspiration. Then she returned to Moscow as Artistic Director of the Russian China and Glass Industry. She was assigned to design perfume bottles for the newly reorganized cosmetics industry, but she was arrested before she could complete the designs.

After her arrest, her many designs were re-attributed to other designers, as it was dangerous to have any association with someone in prison. Secretly, Natalia Danko, Chief Sculptor at Lomonosov, sculpted a porcelain medallion with Eva's profile—and hid it. It was rediscovered, and reproduced, in 2000. While Eva was in prison, one of her Dulevo sets won a Grand Prix at the 1937 Paris International Exposition, but she was never told about it.

• • •

Although we, Eva's family, have heard these wonderful and colorful stories about her experiences in Russia, for many years Eva did not want to make her prison experiences public. She was still traumatized by the memory as well as being afraid that the NKVD would come after her in the U.S. This fear was not far-fetched. But by 1987 she relented.

Suzannah Lessard, who was writing a New Yorker profile about her, convinced her to share some of her prison experiences with the public.

In 2000 Eva was invited to visit the Lomonosov Porcelain Factory in St Petersburg—the same factory where she had worked in the early 1930s. (Ten years earlier she had received an official letter of rehabilitation from the Russian government.) Eva happily accepted the invitation but declared that she was much too old to travel alone, and absolutely needed to be accompanied by her daughter, son-in-law and granddaughter. So we all spent a wonderful two weeks in St. Petersburg.

After touring the factory and participating in a jury of its work, Eva sat down with a young modelmaker named Georgy Bogdevich and started to design an exquisite tea set that is now on the market. It's also in the permanent collection of the Cooper Hewitt National Design Museum.

It was in connection with this Russian trip that we met Dr. Karen Kettering, a lovely lady who is a scholar of Russian art. She had written her thesis on Natalia Danko, the Lomonosov artist who had made the medallion. When we met Karen, she was Curator of Russian and East European Art at the Hillwood Museum, in Washington, DC. Then she became Vice President, Specialist in Russian Works of Art at Sotheby's.

It was Karen who, with great zeal, helped get copies of Eva's Russian KGB file, and who translated and analyzed the interrogation records and other documents. We have incorporated some of the Russian originals, and Karen's translations, into this eBook. Although Eva says her memories have been "gilded by time," these documents confirm the accuracy of her recollections.

Recently, a friend of ours read Eva's prison memoir and found it disingenuous. He did not believe that one could write about such a serious situation with so much humor and charm. But she was not disingenuous. That was Eva. She often felt like a tourist in life, which meant she could look at herself from the outside, in a detached, sometimes bemused way.

Towards the end of 2010 we have made some amazing discoveries about Eva's case. In her memoir, Eva mentions finding a book in the New York Public Library in the late 1950's called The Secret History of Stalin's Crimes, by Alexander Orlov. In this book she saw a reference to her own accuser, Bykhovskii, and to the man who had accused

Bykhovskii. She read that they were all intended to be part of the first show trial.

Years later we had the idea of publishing this eBook and wondered whether there might be additional material about Eva in Orlov's unpublished notes. Through the Internet we found out that Orlov had been a high-up, NKVD general who had defected to the U.S. in 1938. Although Orlov had died in 1973, Edward Gazur, his last FBI handler and debriefer, who became his close friend and executor, was still very much alive. I phoned him at his home in Kentucky, and he answered somewhat warily, in fact a bit gruffly. He never picked up the phone, he said, but his wife happened to have laryngitis. Very politely, I told him about Eva's imprisonment and that we had a few questions he might be able to help us with. "Email me," he said.

There were three mysteries I asked him about. The first was, Who was the man called Nikultsev? Nikultsev was the first person to interrogate Eva after she was imprisoned in Leningrad. He had come from the Kremlin, and Eva's impression was that he really wanted to find out if Stalin's life was in danger from her. Eva describes him as attractive, elegant, soft spoken, highly educated and very nice. They saw each other every evening for over a week in an elegant office, and late at night he would have tea brought in with sandwiches and caviar for them both. He sometimes called his home office in the Kremlin in her presence. Before returning to the Kremlin he ordered some daily hot water for Eva, gave her a newspaper, and told her she must hold her nerves together, as she would have a very hard time. Eva was sure he was convinced of her innocence. The odd thing is that there was no trace of Nikultsev in Eva's Russian files. Whoever he really was, he took all his notes with him. We were sure we would never find out his identity, which was probably buried deep in the bowels of the Kremlin.

The second question was: Did Orlov ever mention Eva's great love, Jascha? Jascha was a general in the NKVD who did undercover work. Eva had met him on a train en route from Berlin to Moscow, while he was traveling as a German businessman. Only later did she find out that he was a general in the Red Army. They fell in love and spent vacations together in Paris and Italy. His full name was Jacob Alexandrovich Ravitch. He was born in Bialystok, and was about ten years older than Eva. He told her that, many years earlier, he had accompanied Stalin to Germany as a "look-out." Stalin, traveling incognito, was shopping for suits in the large Berlin department store, KVD. According to historians, Stalin never left Russia.

Jascha also told Eva about his experiences as an investigator in the 1931 Menshevik trials. He knew his prisoner was innocent, and greatly respected him.[20][2] When his prisoner didn't confess, Jascha was ordered to torture him, but he refused, so Jascha himself was put into prison.

Shortly after Eva was released, she related her prison experiences to her old friend, Arthur Koestler, who incorporated many of these details into his famous novel *Darkness At Noon*. Jascha, for example, became the model for the principal character of Ivanov, the investigator. Until now, the Jascha/Ivanov connection has not been made public.

When Jascha was assigned to travel to the Far East, Eva saw him off from Venice. As they parted, he told her that no one would ever love her as much as he. She recalls that he boarded a hospital ship that had something to do with Spain. He was on his way to Manchuria. From Shanghai, he wrote to Eva via his friend in a Jewish organization in Paris. We wanted to know more about Jascha, and what became of him. At that time we had not yet found Jascha's name on the list of people who were later shot.

The third question was: Why did Gazur think Eva was expelled rather than shot?

Well, Special Agent Gazur certainly solved the first mystery, the true identity of Nikultsev. What he said gave me goosebumps, and I told him so.

From the beginning I had the feeling that Gazur had an idea about the identity of Nikultsev, that he had someone in mind. He asked many detailed questions about him which Eva was able to answer because amazingly—at 104—she remembered Nikultsev very well.

This is what Gazur told us: One day, during their debriefings, Orlov told him about an assignment he had had in the spring of 1936. Orlov had been ordered by Stalin, whom he knew well, to go to Leningrad to interview a young woman who had been arrested, accused of plotting to kill Stalin. She had recently moved to Russia from Germany and, since the interview was conducted in German, Gazur had assumed she was a

---

[20] Identified by Karen Kettering as Abram Ginzburg (1878-1937), sentenced to 10 years imprisonment and 5 years loss of rights, but died in 1937. He was rehabilitated in 1991.

German national. Stalin had sent Orlov to find out if his life was actually in danger from this young woman. Orlov described the woman as attractive, adventurous, Bohemian and tending towards the arts (artistic). He also described her as talking too much for her own good. Orlov told Gazur he had reported to Stalin that, in his opinion, the young lady was innocent. Clearly, the young lady was Eva, and Orlov, himself, was Nikultsev. (At that time Orlov's undercover name was Nikolsky. Whether he introduced himself as Nikultsev, or Eva misremembered it , we do not know.)

It is amazing to see how Orlov's and Eva's narratives mesh. (It's also noteworthy that each described the other as "attractive.") Eva writes that during their interviews she told Nikultsev that she had been in love with Jascha, an NKVD general, who was then on a mission in Manchuria. Nikultsev told her, in essence, to keep her mouth shut. This exchange is surely what Orlov referred to when he told Gazur she had talked too much, telling him more than he needed to hear.

Pondering the revelation about Nikultsev/Orlov, I realized that both Eva and her first investigator came to this country in the same year, 1938, one as an émigré, the other as a defector. What would they have thought had they bumped into each other on the streets of New York, just two years after facing each other in a Russian prison?

About Jascha, Gazur had no notes or recollections, but he was sure that Jascha and Orlov would have known each other and worked together:

I am convinced [writes Gazur] that Orlov and Jascha were friends in the KGB [NKVD]. They probably met in the 1930s in Berlin, or perhaps before. But what really makes me believe they knew each other was the interview Orlov had with Eva when he warned her not to reveal to her investigators that she had a relationship with Jascha. Orlov was protecting Jascha by this means. Had the information gotten out that an NKVD officer had a relationship with a person accused of threatening Stalin, it would have been a sure ticket to Siberia, at best.

Regarding the third question about Eva's fate, Gazur wrote the following to me:

The fact that Orlov was directed to find the truth early on indicated the seriousness of the case against Eva. Notwithstanding his findings, she continued to be held. Had she been a Soviet citizen she would have been shot after a sham trial. In spite of Orlov's findings that the allegation was false, they kept her incarcerated to be on the safe side.

They would have let her rot in jail, at least to the time of the collapse of the Soviet Union...

Besides Orlov's findings that there was no merit to the case against her, Eva has Eva to thank for her fortitude not to crumble under intense pressure to make a false confession. Had she done so, this would have been the end of the journey for Eva. What finally got her released? Here all the credit must go to the tenacity of Eva's mother and Eva's former husband, Alex Weissberg.

While Eva was in prison, her mother and Alex worked heroically to get her out. Alex mobilized many important Russian scientists and academics to write letters vouching for Eva (found in Appendix D). These were some of the top scientists and academicians in the Soviet Union. She had met and socialized with them at Alex's scientific institute in Kharkov. These letters were taken very seriously because, had Eva been shot, the letter-writers would have shared her fate. That was the rule. Her mother and Alex personally delivered copies of these letters to various officials, including the Chief Prosecutor of Leningrad. (Eva was shocked to learn afterwards that her mother appeared before these officials wearing a Tsarist medal her grandfather had received.) Alex writes about their quest in his autobiography, *The Accused*.

Gazur concludes that, with these letters in hand: It came down to a matter of public relations, as now the Soviets had something to lose. By 1937, rumors of Stalin's crimes had started to leak out, and Stalin was very concerned about his reputation. With so many prominent people supporting Eva's release, the Soviets had little choice. Stalin did not want more negative, foreign publicity. (In conversation with Gazur.)

At first, Stalin's concern with publicity sounded very superficial to me. Why would a man who had committed such horrendous crimes be worried about public relations? I have since learned that there is a deep conviction in the Russian character that it is a terrible thing to air one's dirty laundry in public. I remember a conversation I once had with a Russian émigré taxi driver just after the Watergate scandal. He was deeply pained by the publicity surrounding the events: "I know it's terrible, you know it's terrible, but why do we have to tell the whole world it's terrible?"

Among the documents in Eva's NKVD file is a letter signed by Andrei Vyshinskii, the Chief Prosecutor of the USSR, essentially reversing a near-certain death penalty. Gazur feels he would not have written this without orders from Stalin:

I don't believe that even the head of the KGB had the authority to release Eva. However, because of Stalin's personal involvement, this means that Stalin understood the message and authorized Eva's release.

● ● ●

We and the Gazurs felt closely connected through General Orlov, and became good friends. Had Orlov not interviewed my mother and reported to Stalin that she was innocent, I surely would not be here today.

My husband, Brent, and I spent a warm weekend with Ed and Ruth Gazur at their home in Kentucky. After dinner on our last night he presented me with a gift box and said: "We feel General Orlov would want you to have this. It's a necklace he bought for his wife, in Paris, in 1926. After she died, he gave it to Ruth, and she wants you to keep it." I burst into tears at the table. Ed writes: "At that moment I could feel General Orlov telling us 'You did the right thing.'"

Appendix B: Behind The Scenes

by Karen Kettering, Ph.D.

For many years, Eva Zeisel struggled to make sense of what she had experienced in the last sixteen months of almost five years living in the Soviet Union. Why, after her long imprisonment, had she been freed and permitted to live when so many others in her same situation had been summarily shot? When she discovered Alexander Orlov's 1953 The Secret History of Stalin's Crimes on the shelves of the New York Public Library, she felt that she had at last uncovered a rational explanation for her arrest. Zeisel instinctively trusted the author's account because many of the details matched what she had learned of the workings of the NKVD from her lover, Yakov Ravich (Jascha). As Orlov explained, Stalin aimed to consolidate his power by permanently eliminating potential rivals, among them the venerable founders of the Bolshevik Party and heroes of the October 1917 Revolution. After the assassination of Leningrad party boss Sergei Kirov on December 1, 1934, Soviet citizens were informed that his death was part of a terrible conspiracy.[21][1] In the months after Kirov's death, Stalin sought to create evidence of additional (invented) conspiracies; specifically, that Stalin's former political rival, Leon Trotsky, was directing clandestine groups of terrorists to infiltrate the Soviet Union and attack the state's leaders. (Trotsky had formed a group opposing Stalin's leadership within the party but was ultimately unsuccessful; he was expelled from the Politburo in 1926 and spent several years in internal exile in Kazakhstan before being deported from the USSR in 1929.) "Evidence" of these conspiracies was presented to the public in a series of show trials in which the party's former leaders (and Trotsky's former allies) were "revealed" as spies, saboteurs, assassins, and traitors. Orlov's book also

---

[21] Although Orlov believed that Stalin had effected Kirov's assassination as a pretext for the murder of his rivals, the event – and whether Stalin had caused it to happen—has remained a controversial topic and the subject of numerous publications. See, most recently, Iu. N. Zhukov, "Sledstvie i sudebnye protsessy po delu ob ubiistve Kirova," Voprosy istorii, no. 2 (2000), 33-51; J. Arch Getty and Oleg V. Naumov, Yezhov: The Rise of Stalin's "Iron Fist" (New Haven: Yale University Press, 2008), 133-155; and, Matthew E. Lenoe, The Kirov Murder and Soviet History (New Haven: Yale University Press, 2010).

contained an extended description of the conspiracy in which Eva had been accused of taking part. Orlov even mentioned by name Mikhail Bykhovskii, Eva's former colleague whose accusation had led to her arrest.[22][2]

That the NKVD had attempted to create a role for her as part of one of the many spurious conspiracies to destroy the Soviet Union was clear, but why did they fail to follow through on this plan? Why was she instead allowed to languish in solitary confinement, virtually ignored, until she was suddenly expelled on September 17, 1937?

With the opening of Soviet archives under the government's program of glasnost (openness) in the second half of the 1980s, Soviet historians and journalists began a public reexamination of the mass arrests and executions of the Stalin era. Public pressure to redress the wrongs of the period grew and on January 16, 1989, the Supreme Soviet of the USSR published a decree reversing the majority of the NKVD's prosecutions of Soviet and foreign citizens. Zeisel, among the millions who were officially "rehabilitated," began the lengthy bureaucratic process of acquiring copies of files pertaining to her arrest, investigation, and expulsion from the Soviet Union. The files were housed in the archives of the KGB, as the successor organization to the NKVD had been renamed in 1954, and could only be released under restricted circumstances. The effort to get photocopies of the full text stretched out over a decade, and was finally successful in 2000. I spent another year translating them and researching and identifying the people and organizations included on their pages.

The texts were something of a shock. Rather than providing a neat explanation for the reasoning behind the decision to free Zeisel, they were arcane and opaque, written in the stilted and formulaic language of official Soviet discourse of the mid-1930s. The only clues were in the other names appearing in Zeisel's file, her alleged co-conspirators, and what I could glean about their fates from other sources. The two key figures turned out to be Valentin Olberg and Mikhail Bykhovskii. Like so many others, Zeisel's arrest was the result of a chance acquaintance. On

---

[22] Orlov's account is based on his recollection of interrogation reports he had read almost twenty years earlier and, unsurprisingly, he did not always recall details accurately. He described "two brothers by the name of Bykhovsky, chemists by education, [who had been] accused falsely of making bombs for the terrorists"; Mikhail and Adolf Bykhovsky were actually cousins. See Alexander Orlov, *The Secret History of Stalin's Crimes* (New York: Random House, 1953), 77

January 5, 1936, NKVD agents arrested Olberg, a newly hired professor of history at a teachers college in a provincial city. (Zeisel had never met him.) The NKVD selected the luckless Olberg to serve as the key figure in a spurious conspiracy that would "prove" Trotsky's attempts to attack the Soviet Union and its leaders. While still living in Europe, Olberg had briefly corresponded with Trotsky and his son, Lev Sedov. (The NKVD apparently knew of this correspondence through an unnamed agent working for Trotsky.) In the hands of Stalin and his colleagues, this brief connection became the basis for a so-called United Anti-Soviet Trotskyite-Zinovievite Center, and the first of the great show trials of the late 1930s. When the prosecution delivered its summation, it was "established" that Trotsky had sent Olberg to the Soviet Union and that he "trained a number of terrorists who were to commit a terroristic act against the leaders of the Soviet Government and the Communist Party of the Soviet Union." Olberg and his co-defendants were sentenced to death and immediately shot.

While still under interrogation early in 1936, Valentin Olberg agreed to admit his own guilt, perhaps in hopes of freeing his wife, Betty, and brother, Paul, both of whom had been arrested with him.[23][3] In a technique that would be used frequently and with devastating consequences during the Great Terror, Olberg was questioned about his friends and associates, and other foreign citizens now living and working in the Soviet Union. This group of foreigners, whether they were Communists who had come to help build socialism or simply looking for employment in the midst of the Depression, was recast as his co-conspirators. His family had spent considerable time in Riga, Latvia during his youth and this appears to be the source of the connection between Olberg and a Latvian engineer named Mikhail Bykhovskii, Zeisel's accuser and former colleague at the Lomonosov Porcelain Factory.

Based on Olberg's coerced statements, Mikhail Bykhovskii was arrested in April 1936 and underwent repeated interrogations. He falsely implicated many of his German-speaking acquaintances and

---

[23] Orlov characterizes him as a "secret agent of the NKVD." While he might have unwittingly provided information to Soviet agents while living abroad, he was not an employee of the organization. A recently published biography gives a more accurate account of his life and the role he played in the show trials. See Vsevolod Vikhnovich, "Sud'ba sem'i Ol'bergov (Mezhdu dvumia mifami)," *Iz glubinyi vremen: almanakh*, no. 9 (1997), 131-13

colleagues, including Zeisel and her modelmaker, Hermann Fuhlbrügge, who had traveled from Berlin to work with the designer. Excerpts from his interrogation conducted on May 20, 1936 and inserted in her file outline a series of chillingly absurd accusations: that Bykhovskii had detected her hostility to the Soviet regime by her reaction to party leaders' speeches and had recruited her to a "foreign Trotskyite center"; that Zeisel had arranged for the Lomonosov State Porcelain Factory to hire Fuhlbrügge [whom she had never met] because she knew him to be a Trotskyite who could be helpful in their attempts on Soviet power; and that, although Bykhovskii had wanted the pair to remain in Leningrad and help him assassinate Kirov, they had insisted on no less a target than Stalin himself. According to Bykhovksii, they had accepted new jobs at the Dulevo Porcelain Factory outside of Moscow in April 1934 not because of the much higher wages and better working conditions, but because this would put her closer to Moscow and facilitate her plans to kill Stalin.

Early in the morning on May 27, 1936, Zeisel was arrested and charged with "counterrevolutionary Trotskyist activities," specifically Articles 58-10 and 58-11 of the Russian Soviet criminal code. (Trotsky's surname was never capitalized in Soviet documents in the period as a not-so-subtle insult.) These were certainly serious charges; 58-10 described "propaganda or agitation, containing a call for the overthrow, subversion, or weakening of Soviet authority or for the carrying out of other counterrevolutionary crimes…" The second charge of having violated Article 58-11 was far more ominous; by applying its seemingly vague language ("any type of membership in a counterrevolutionary organization"), the state indicated that it officially considered the accused to be a terrorist and an "enemy of the people" (vrag naroda). Conviction under these statutes typically resulted in sentences of three to ten years in the camps. As any number of memoirs of the period have shown, detention in the camps, depending on its location and condition, could be a death sentence.

Throughout, Zeisel steadfastly refused to give false testimony, never admitting the serious charges Bykhovskii had leveled against her, i.e., that she had participated in a terrorist group intending to assassinate Stalin. After weeks of incarceration, however, Zeisel did briefly let her guard down when she was informed that the investigation was coming to an end. Elias Shmalts, the young officer in charge of her case, told her, falsely,

> ...if you deny everything we will accuse you of the whole volume of your accusation. ... If, for example, you admit that you knew Bykhovskii was an enemy of the people, you will get two years or you will be sent out of the country. Nothing much can happen to you because you are a foreigner. But if you say that you did not even know he was an enemy, and you did not have any conversations with him, you will be accused of everything. We can accept that he exaggerated, but not that he invented the accusation.

On August 5, 1936, Zeisel briefly admitted to knowing that Bykhovskii was a Trotskyist and that she had witnessed him making counter-revolutionary statements without reporting them to the authorities. The shocked expression on Shmalts' face caused her to realize that he had lied to her and that this limited false declaration had been a terrible mistake. This led to her suicide attempt and, within a week, she recanted the confession and insisted that she be permitted to insert a final statement in her file. In this statement, handwritten in German, Zeisel asserted that Bykhovskii's accusations could not be true. For example, he had asserted that their conversations took place in Zeisel's room in the hotel where they had both lived but, during the only period in which this could have taken place, he was living in the October Hotel and she in the Astoria. Nevertheless, when the NKVD summarized its case against her in August 1936 they continued to assert that she had had "counterrevolutionary Trotskyist conversations" with Bykhovskii, but no longer accused her of attempting to organize a terrorist attack on the life of Stalin.

After Kirov's assassination [December, 1934], the government rapidly passed a series of draconian new regulations allowing those accused of terrorism to be tried in abbreviated proceedings and immediately executed. In 2002, the Russian government published 383 lists of names held in the top-secret Archive of the President of the Russian Federation. These lists, which included more than 44,000 names of persons sentenced to death by the Military Collegium of the Soviet Supreme Court, had been sent to Stalin and the members of the Politburo for their approval. The earliest two lists record the names of 114 persons living in or near Leningrad who were shot on October 10 and 11, 1936. A careful reading of that list indicates that Mikhail Bykhovskii and everyone he had accused (with the exception of Zeisel and Fuhlbrügge) had been shot.[24][4] From our contemporary vantage point, this particular spasm of violence is one of the starting points of the Great Terror and it is shocking to see how perilously close Zeisel was to being swept away.

Zeisel had long suspected that her release was to due to the efforts of her mother, Laura Polanyi Striker, and her first husband, the physicist Alexander Weissberg. (Weissberg was himself arrested by the NKVD on March 1, 1937.) In his memoir, published in the United States under the title The Accused, Weissberg recalled their efforts:

[After Zeisel's arrest] her mother and I had done everything possible to help her. We had applied to the Military Prosecutor in Leningrad and to the General Prosecutor [Procurator] in Moscow. At first the whole thing had appeared quite hopeless, but gradually we had worked our way through the maze until finally we had reached the official who had my wife's case in hand. We had collected written declarations in her favor, and a number of members of the Academy of Science had been prepared to come forward on her behalf. [...] My mother-in-law knew all the intricacies of Soviet legal procedure. An ordinary Soviet citizen, and still more so a foreigner, would not even know to whom to address himself.[25][5]

Weissberg's recollections give only the barest sense of the confusion of overlapping jurisdictions that characterized the Soviet legal system, particularly as the government attempted to address the cases of thousands of citizens arrested in the wake of the Kirov assassination and the alleged conspiracies then being "uncovered." Several extrajudicial organizations were formed to deal with the increased number of defendants. As these organizations and their responsibilities proliferated, an increasingly acrimonious battle broke out between the NKVD and the Procuracy (Prokuratura). Officially, this office, headed by Chief Procurator of the USSR Andrei Vyshinskii, was tasked with supervising the observance of the law by all government organizations, including the NKVD and military justice organs. Indeed, when the NKVD finished its investigation of Zeisel, the office of the Leningrad Procuracy would review the findings and charges. Not surprisingly, the NKVD staff

---

[24] Archive of the President of the Russian Federation, opis 24, file 413, pp. 373-74. See stable URL at Stalin memo.

[25] Alexander Weissberg, The Accused (trans. Edward Fitzgerald) (New York: Simon and Schuster, 1951), 66.

resented this oversight, particularly when it seemed that hidden enemies beset the country.[26][6]

Perhaps because of the vast number of arrestees crowding Soviet prisons, or because of the delicate treatment a case concerning two foreign citizens required, the Procuracy staff did not review the file until December 1936, some four months after the completion of the investigation. Whatever the reason, they treated the matter with unusual care. It was reviewed not in Leningrad, but in Moscow by the office of Chief Procurator Vyshinskii. On December 11, his Deputy, Grigorii Leplevskii, probably writing on Vyshinskii's behalf, wrote to the head of their Leningrad office outlining the holes in the NKVD's case, and asking him to further investigate these points and report back as soon as possible. Shpigel, a young assistant procurator in the Leningrad office, spent several days re-interviewing Zeisel and Fuhlbrügge, confirming their whereabouts and movements against hotel registries, and having the letters collected by Alex Weissberg and Laura Striker officially inserted into the NKVD file. A cover note written by a senior administrator in the Leningrad Prosecutor's office, dated December 29, 1936, suggests that the NKVD investigators had not wanted the letters included in the official record and that the Prosecutor's staff was forced to insist on their addition: "The declaration of Citizen Weissberg and documents (nine pages total) were received personally by comrade Shpigel and he ordered that it be included in the file."

The following Monday, January 5, 1937, Vyshinskii himself wrote to Yakov Aggrenox, Deputy Director of the NKVD, instructing that Zeisel and Fuhlbrügge's case should be reviewed by the NKVD's Special Committee (osoboe soveshchanie).

The Special Committee was an extrajudicial panel located in Moscow which operated in parallel with other courts, determining sentences for political criminals accused of counterrevolutionary agitation, terrorism, or conspiring to commit acts of terrorism. When Zeisel was arrested in the spring of 1936, Vyshinskii was attempting to limit the powers of the Special Committee because, as he complained to Stalin in a memo, its members made their decisions after hearing only oral summaries of

---

[26] Paul Hagenloh, Stalin's Police: Public Order and Mass Repression in the USSR, 1936-1941 (Baltimore: The Johns Hopkins University Press, 2009), 209-214.

cases without the presence of the accused or witnesses.[27][7] (The accused also had no representation, but the lack of defense lawyers troubled Vyshinskii less than the absence of defendants or witnesses. Despite such glaring drawbacks, the Special Committee at this time was a relatively more attractive option for the accused because its members could not sentence persons to long terms of confinement or, more importantly, to death. (This would not be the case from 1941-1945.) It also had the power to expel "dangerous" foreigners; this might have been the source of the enticing offer Investigator Shmalts had made that caused Zeisel to sign a false confession, which she quickly recanted.

Documents in Zeisel's file show that the officers of the NKVD were unwilling to acquiesce to the demands of Vyshinskii that they decide her fate themselves.[28][8] When the NKVD's Special Committee examined Zeisel and Fuhlbrügge's case on February 14, 1937, the members chose to transfer the case to the Military Collegium of the Supreme Court of the USSR.

This judicial body considered cases of unusual importance, including those of persons accused of treason and counterrevolutionary activity. Trials were overseen by three judges and generally lasted no longer than five to ten minutes. As with the Special Committee, the defendant was not present and had no representation. The Military Collegium meted out sentences to those whose names appeared on special lists prepared by the NKVD and personally approved by Stalin and a select group of members of the Politburo.[29][9] In 1937, only three sorts of sentences were handed out: the great majority of defendants received the death penalty, while the minority was sentenced to either ten or eight years in the camps.

The process by which the Soviet government investigated and punished suspected "spies, traitors, and saboteurs" offered the accused little protection, but the officers of the NKVD did have to adhere to a system of regulations. Those regulations demanded that Zeisel's case

---

[27] N.S. Plotnikova, "O deiatel'nosti osobogo soveshchanie pri NKVD SSSR," in *Istoricheskie chtenia na Lubianke* 1999 god: *Otechestvennye spetssluzhby* v 20-30-e gody, (Moscow, 2000) and Hagenloh, Stalin's Police, 214-216.

[28] J. Arch Getty and Oleg V. Naumov, *The Road to Terror: Stalin and the Self-Destruction of the Bolsheviks*, 1932-1939 (New Haven: Yale University Press, 1999), 273.

[29] Marc Jansen and Nikita Petrov, "Mass Terror and the Court: The Military Collegium of the USSR," *Europe-Asia Studies* vol. 58, no. 4 (June 2006), 589-602.

could not be transferred to the Military Collegium without first being reexamined by Vyshinskii's office. And here we find that the remaining documents cannot answer all of our questions. There are no letters or memos to explain what took place between February 14, when the NKVD's Special Committee decided to send the case to the Military Collegium, and March 8, when Vyshinskii's deputy Leplevskii wrote the NKVD, addressing the memo to Deputy Director Mikhail Frinovskii and saying that, "in accordance with your agreement with Comrade Vyshinskii" Zeisel's case should be sent back to the (less powerful) Special Committee because "further inspection of the case leads to the conclusion that it is impossible to examine judicially [i.e., for her to be sent to the Military Collegium]."

It is highly probable that Stalin personally intervened in the case; when Vyshinskii and the NKVD came into conflict, as they had in Zeisel's case, both sides appealed to the leader and other highly placed members of the Politburo for resolution. Stalin preferred to intervene in such matters orally and few traces remain of these conversations.[30][10] So why would he have intervened? Certainly, the fact that Zeisel and Fuhlbrügge were foreigners was helpful, but the lists of names of persons whose execution Stalin and other Politburo members approved is dotted with notations that the executed were foreign citizens. It is very probable that the packet of letters collected by Alex Weissberg and Laura Striker helped to sway Stalin's actions in Zeisel's favor, although it is difficult to provide a brief or neat explanation. We cannot say that Stalin feared angering some of his nation's most talented scientists; many scientific institutions were being drawn into the purges and talented physicists, including Weissberg and Houtermanns (who were also foreign citizens), were later arrested and occasionally executed. Certainly the number and prominence of the scientists who were willing to take the dangerous step of vouching for her must have stood out. Although the NKVD's investigation files remain largely classified, published excerpts indicate that vouching for an accused individual was an extraordinarily rare phenomenon. The testimonials of such prominent individuals surely were noted as the insistence of Vyshinskii's

---

[30] I am grateful to Professor J. Arch Getty of UCLA for examining key documents from Zeisel's file and discussing them in context of his extensive research on this period. Personal communication to author, August 13, 2002.

staff shows. Surely Vyshinskii mentioned their existence in any conversations he had with Stalin concerning the matter.

Finally, we must consider Zeisel's remarkable display of will. Many of the arrested willingly signed absurd confessions in an attempt to save spouses or children. Others succumbed to a system in which physical and psychological isolation were carefully calibrated to induce panic and acquiescence. Zeisel realized that to give in to this panic was immeasurably dangerous:

> The way they try to break you is by breaking your dignity. The minute your dignity is gone you are lost. So I made a point of keeping my dignity. ...[When I sat opposite Shmalts], I was sitting straight. One day his colleague came by and he said, "What can I do with her? Look at her, look how she sits!"

Her resilience and her refusal to be intimidated, even in these terrifying circumstances, cannot be underestimated as part of the reason for her release. She understood that the situation was terrifying, but in the absence of "righteousness ... I understood that it was I who was now my whole world. In me was all the power for beauty and dignity and strength, and I sat down on my bench and started to think a beautiful thought."

Appendix C: A Case Solved

by FBI Special Agent Edward P. Gazur

I was a career Special Agent of the FBI, specializing in Eastern European espionage and counterespionage and was selected for one of the most fascinating assignments of the cold war: to protect and debrief the highest ranking defector of all time, KGB General Alexander Orlov. Despite our different backgrounds and having worked for opposing intelligence services we became friends and the old Bolshevik entrusted many secrets to his FBI confidant. My relationship with General Orlov began when I first met him on August 17, 1971 in Cleveland, Ohio, and ended with his death on April 7, 1973.

Never in the world had I ever expected to be in touch with someone who actually had contact with the late KGB General way back in 1936. Ironically, this person, who spent a week with General Orlov in 1936, did not know his true identity, and it was not until I put two and two together that the truth came out.

Sometime in mid-July, 2010 I received a telephone call from a lady who identified herself as Jean Richards. Normally my incoming telephone calls are screened by my wife, but on this particular occasion she was incapacitated with laryngitis and I had to take the call. I was somewhat reluctant to take the call, but as the caller carried on, I became fascinated by what she had to say. My FBI training dictated that I remain blasé and aloof to the matter.

She related that she was from the New York City area and was doing research for a book about her mother, Eva Zeisel, dealing with her mother's incarceration in the Soviet Union in 1936 on charges that she conspired to assassinate Soviet Dictator Josef Stalin. Her mother had read Orlov's first book published in 1953 The Secret History of Stalin's Crimes, and was amazed to find that her accuser on the conspiracy charges was named in the book. This led to the question of what else General Orlov knew and how it might relate to Zeisel's case. Further research by Ms. Richards revealed that I was not only the last handler of Orlov, his close friend and his executor, but I had also written a book about him: Secret Assignment: The FBI'S KGB General.[1] dealing with my association with General Orlov.

As she went on to tell me about the tragic events during Stalin's Great Purges that impacted her mother, I became ever more interested and glued my ear to the telephone receiver. The events she spoke of were those I had learned of early on from General Orlov. Richards was very sincere in her presentation and I was most impressed by her dedication to her mother by going the extra mile. How could you not help this lady who made such an eloquent plea for information on behalf of her mother? I told her to put everything she told me into an email.

After I left the telephone, I kept thinking of what she had said about her mother's imprisonment during Stalin's Great Purges and how she escaped the death penalty. The more I thought of these details the more I realized I had been down the same road many years ago.

It didn't take Richards long to get back to me. The most salient question to me was in regards to a KGB Official who interviewed Zeisel while she was incarcerated at the KGB Bolshoi Dom Prison, in Leningrad. She knew him by the name of Nikultsev.

Richards' question in the email was: "Who was Nikultsev?" She gave extensive background information to help identify this person. When I first read her email, certain aspects of the narrative hit home. When I read it further, and measured its contents against what I already knew, it immediately became apparent to me that the KGB Official by the name of Nikultsev had to be General Orlov himself. But I wanted more confirmation, so I posed more detailed questions to Richards.

My wife is privy to this matter and knew General Orlov very well. I handed this particular question to her with the only comment that it was interesting and she should read it. After reading the contents of the question and the related information she handed back the page with the comment, "it sounds like General Orlov."

What brought it all together for me was one of my regular debriefing conversations with Orlov early in the 1970s. My major debriefing of Orlov took place in the evenings, at my residence, for security reasons. After supper, Orlov and I would retreat downstairs to the Bavarian Room. Here I would interview him using a large trestle table as a desk. One evening, when we were discussing tactics to obtain confessions from political dissidents, he told me of a matter he had handled during the spring of 1936. This was a priority matter personally requested by Dictator Stalin. The KGB had arrested a young woman charged with threatening the life of Stalin. The basis of the arrest was a tip from a fellow worker [According to Richards, Eva's accuser had been an engineer in the Lomonosov Factory when Eva worked there]. Stalin wanted Orlov to make an independent judgment as to the merits of the case. The lady in question was not a Soviet National, and had last resided in Germany. One has to realize that Stalin was paranoid when it came to the Germans. He always believed they were out to get him, and he was correct. Any threat against him was taken very seriously, and Eva's case was no exception, more so because of her residency in Germany

Our discussion took place many years ago, and I don't recall all of the details. What I do recall clearly is that there was a great concern that the lady was a threat, and that the matter had to be expeditiously resolved. In the end, Orlov concluded that the allegation was false, and that the lady told the truth. His final report to Stalin exonerated her.

Back to Eva's responses to the questions I posed to her. One of the key issues was the language used in the interview. Orlov spoke fluent German and handled the interview in German. This was just another factor that indicated that Orlov conducted the interview. Eva's assessment that her interrogator was very educated, spoke nicely, wore gentleman's clothing, was elegant, slim and attractive, fit Orlov to a T.

Orlov related to me that the lady was somewhat attractive and appealing to him. She was definitely the "Bohemian' type. Her life was adventurous, she had traveled extensively, and she was inclined towards the arts. When he told me he had interviewed her in German, I assumed she was a German national. He also felt she was far too open for her own good, as she volunteered more information than he wanted to know. He felt this might lead to her downfall. He thought she had probably stepped on someone's foot, and that that person had taken revenge by means of the allegation against her.

Following our official debriefing, Orlov and I would go into a more social mode, where we discussed more pleasant, social matters over a glass of his favorite liqueur, Drambuie. That night he surprised me when he again brought up the matter of the lady that he had spoken about previously. This was most unusual, as we hardly ever overlapped the official and the social parts of our evenings. So I had to suspect there was more to the story. He went on to say the lady was of strong character and on the attractive side, which was to his liking. From the few remarks he made I was left with the impression that he may have been somewhat infatuated with her.

Eva's recollection of the man who interviewed her was that he was decent, quiet and really a nice person. Sometimes at midnight he would order fine food including caviar for both of them. This would be the Orlov I knew. Only a top KGB general would have the authority to do this.

Eva was finally released from her incarceration by the Soviets in September 1937 some 16 months after her arrest. By this time General Orlov was in Spain up to his neck in work, and yet he must have inquired about her fate, because he told me he knew she had been released.

I have to wonder what KGB General Orlov would think had he known that, through a strange set of circumstances 74 years after the fact, I had contact with the lady whom he interviewed in the KGB prison in Leningrad, way back in 1936. No doubt he would be as flabbergasted as I was.

Endnotes

[G1] Edward P. Gazur, Secret Assignment: The FBI's KGB General (London: St. Erman's Press and Little, Brown & Company, 2001. New York: Carroll and Graf Publishers, 2002).

General Orlov's Background

by   Edward P. Gazur

As with all stories, we have to start at the beginning in a more peaceful Russia. Leiba (Leon) Lazaravich Feldbin was born on 12 August 1895 in the rural town of Bobruysk, in the Byelorussia district of Russia. His parents were both Jewish and strongly dedicated to their religion.

During his long career with the KGB Feldbin used well over 50 aliases but the one the world would identify with was the name Alexander

Orlov and to the world of intelligence it was also his code name, Schwed.

During the early phase of the Great War the Feldbin family moved to Moscow where the young Leon was admitted to the esteemed Lazarevsky Institute because of his superior intelligence. On graduation he was admitted to the Moscow University's prestigious School of Law. In the fall of 1916 he was drafted into the Tsar's Army where he served as a private far from the battlefield. Orlov's education, background and strong character would dictate that he be an officer in the Imperial Army but such was not the case. Jews were not accepted for officer training nor were they assigned to the prime units but rather relegated to the infantry or clerical positions in support units.

History would be changed forever when the first shots of the two Russian Revolutions echoed in St. Petersburg, Russia in February 1917. The path to the revolution started as a consequence of World War I when the seeds of discontent were first spawned. As the war dragged on and losses mounted the Russian people became more and more discontent and under the provocations of the socialistic movement in the country took to the streets to protest the government of Czar Nicholas II. Within days the back of the Monarchy was broken and Czar Nicolas II was forced to abdicate. A Provisional Government was set in place and in July 1918 the Czar and his family were murdered by elements of the Provisional Government.

The second Russian Revolution soon followed in October of 1917 when the Bolsheviks under the leadership Vladimir Lenin outmaneuvered the principal leaders of the Provisional Government and after seizing power sued for peace under the accords of the Brest-Litovsk Treaty of 1918 thus ending the Russian participation in the Great War. The situation of Orlov changed quite drastically under the new regime when the barriers towards Jews were broken and he was able to enter Officers training and graduate as a second lieutenant in March 1917. In May of that year he joined the Bolshevik Party under the name Lev Lazaravich Nikol'skiy.

The success of the October Revolution and the end of open hostilities in the Great War permitted Orlov to return to civilian life. Again historical events interceded when civil war broke out in 1918 when the Russian White Armies consolidated their efforts to overthrow the Bolshevik Government and restore the Monarchy. Orlov felt he had no choice but to help the cause of the Bolsheviks by reentering the Red

Army. During the spring of 1920 Poland invaded Russia with much success. The White Russian Armies took this opportunity to achieve their mutual objective to overthrow the Bolshevik Government. As a consequence Orlov was posted to the 12th Red Army fighting along the Polish front in September 1920.

This was Orlov's first encounter with counterintelligence and guerrilla warfare when he was given command of a detachment that operated behind the Polish lines. His ingenious planning strategies and personally led bold operations behind enemy lines soon brought him to the personal attention of Felix Dzerzhinsky, Chairman of the Checka (forerunner of the KGB).

Within the context of this historical framework we can now follow the events that led to Alexander Orlov's rise to the zenith of power in the KGB. The days, months and years of the two Russian Revolutions were indeed a period of turbulence as well as a period of hope for the future. These were the heady days of all those Dr. Zhivagos out there whose stories end shortly after the solidification of the revolutions and the Orlov saga only begins.

Orlov married his wife Maria on 1 April 1921 while both were serving with the Red Army. In time she too would become connected with the KGB as a trusted courier. They had a daughter Veronika, called Vera, who was born 1 September 1923 in Moscow and died 15 July 1940 in Los Angeles, California as a result of a recurring illness. This was their only child.

In the fall of 1921, the Orlovs were released from the Red Army and returned to Moscow where Orlov reentered law school on a part time basis. In spite of Orlov's limited legal qualifications he was a trusted member of the Communist Party and as such was appointed an Assistant Prosecutor in the Collegiums of Appeals of the Soviet Supreme Court where he was involved in writing the Soviet's original criminal code.

Early in 1924, Orlov graduated from the Moscow University School of Law. His impressive record at the Collegiums of Appeals did not go unnoticed by Dzerzhinsky, who remembered his protégé from his earlier escapades during the revolution. In 1924 Dszerzhinsky brought Orlov into the OGPU, the forerunner of the KGB, as a Deputy Director in the Economic Directorate. Orlov served in Moscow for about a year and in 1925 was appointed a brigade commander of the OGPU Border Guard stationed in Tiflis, Transcaucasia. It was here that he first came in contact with the infamous Lavrenti Beria, then Deputy Director of the OGPU in Georgia, USSR, who in later years became the dreaded head of the KGB.

In early 1926 Orlov was recalled to the Headquarters of the KGB, known as the Center, to head a department of the newly organized Foreign Department (INO). The INO controlled the Soviet's spy activities around the world. Here, Orlov seized on an opportunity for a foreign assignment and with the recommendation of Dzerzhinsky, Orlov was posted to the Soviet Embassy in Paris in mid 1926 under a false identity and the cover of an accredited Soviet diplomat to the Soviet Trade Delegation. Actually, Orlov was the chief of the legal *rezidentura* at the Embassy who controlled the Soviet spy rings in France.

In the same time frame, and of particular interest to the British people is the KGB's version of how Sidney Reilly, perhaps Britain's most famous spy and the subject of the 1983 television series "Reilly, Ace of Spies", was lured to the USSR with the help of a mole within MI6 and executed. In his twilight years Orlov revealed the identity of the mole who betrayed Reilly's trust. This revelation caused quite a stir in England as reflected in an August 21, 2001 article appearing in the *Sunday Times* (London). Historians have long debated the final fate of Reilly, the consensus believing he was executed by the KGB and the skeptics believing him to have languished in a KGB prison. Orlov was able to put the final piece of the puzzle into place in 1936 when the KGB Officer who assassinated Reilly became his subordinate in Spain.

As to Dzerzhinsky, he died within a matter of weeks after handing Orlov his Paris assignment. However, he became the symbol of the collapse of the Soviet Government long after his death when TV showed footage around the world of the huge bronze statute of Dzerzhinsky being toppled off its pedestal in front of the old KGB Lubyanka Headquarters in Moscow by jubilant protestors.

Berlin was the spy capitol of Europe and it was there that the KGB placed its best resources. In this instance it was Orlov who had set the standard in France and who again was called upon to head the Soviet's spy efforts in pre- Hitler Germany. Again he was dispatched as a Soviet diplomat but under the fictitious identity of Lev Lazarevich Feldel, a name he had no problem remembering as it was so similar to his real name.

Espionage in Germany proved to be a harder nut to crack with more failures than successes due to the relentless efforts of the elite German

Intelligence Service (GIS). Orlov sensed that the KGB's modus operandi was outdated as the GIS had only to focus on Soviet Embassy personnel to figure out which diplomats actually were working for the KGB. He felt that the KGB should work independently of the Embassy to make the detection effort more difficult but on the other hand realized that without the benefit of the legal cover of a diplomat the work would thus become enormously dangerous. Orlov proposed his idea to the KGB Center which in turn recognized Orlov as the man who could transform the service. With the GIS breathing down his neck Orlov was recalled to Moscow in April 1931 where he would implement his ideas. From that day hence Orlov concentrated his efforts in the new direction and traveled to every capitol in Europe to discuss the new focus and policy with the chiefs of the various legal *rezidenturas*. New codes, dead drops and means of communications between the KGB Center and illegal residents in the field had to be developed.

It was during this period that the KGB credits Orlov with the recruitment and development of the infamous British traitors known as the Cambridge Spy Ring, to wit: Kim Philby, Donald Maclean, Guy Burgess, Anthony Blunt et al., and acknowledged him as the KGB's Master Spy.

The pinnacle of his KGB career was reached in August 1936 when the Soviet Politburo hand-picked General Orlov and with the personal approval of Soviet Dictator Josef Stalin appointed him the personal representative of the Soviet Government to the Spanish Republican Government at the inception of the Spanish Civil War. In this capacity General Orlov had vast powers that exceeded the Soviet military and diplomatic corps in Spain during this tumultuous period in history.

Perhaps the General's most famous achievement came early in the Spanish Civil War when the General masterminded the theft by deception of two thirds of the gold reserves of Spain that was in the hands of the Republicans. Not an easy task by any means as the gold was contained in almost 8,000 wooden crates each weighing 145 pounds. On today's market the value of a troy ounce of gold being well in excess of $1,500, this would amount to billions upon billions of American dollars making this caper the largest heist in history.

When Generalissimo Franco was about to take Republican held Madrid the gold was moved from the Bank of Spain to naval ammunition storage caves just north of Cartagena. Early on the Republican President, Prime Minister and Finance Minister recognized that in time the gold could fall into the hands of Franco and considered the possibility of the Soviet Union as a safe haven for the gold. Orlov was under the personal orders of Stalin to see to it that the gold would be transferred to the Soviet Union without any intention of it ever being returned to Spain. The risky plan was carried out in an air tight shroud of secrecy as the slightest rumor or hint that Spain's gold reserves were being shipped to the Soviet Union would result in an uprising the magnitude of which would not only kill the plan but the conspirators. Orlov personally supervised the transfer of the gold reserves from the caves to the port of Cartagena where he had commandeered 4 Soviet Cargo vessels. Over a period of 3 nights utilizing 20 Soviet heavy military trucks Orlov managed to move the gold to the Soviet vessels which departed Cartagena on October 26, 1936. The vessels had to elude a blockade in the Mediterranean Sea but made it safely to Odessa.

Stalin was beside himself when the gold arrived in the USSR and he made it quite clear that Spain would never again see their gold reserves. To this day the matter remains a bone of contention although there is no likelihood that the gold reserves will ever be returned. One of the most profound, tragic and unsolved mysteries of the Spanish Civil War was the aerial bombardment of the German pocket battleship *Deutschland* as it was lying at anchor just off the island of Ibiza in the Mediterranean on May 29, 1937, resulting in the death of 23 German sailors. The Germans retaliated with warships that shelled the Republican held town of Almeria, Spain resulting in the deaths of 20 civilians and destruction of some of the city's finest buildings. The implications were so far reaching at the time that a strong possibility existed that the incident would be a provocation for the start of World War II, a full two years before the actual event. The true instigator of the attack on the *Deutschland* and the rationale behind the aggression was never absolutely confirmed, although suspicion abounded in many directions. Not until the publication of the author's book were the mysterious circumstances surrounding the incident revealed for the first time that the KGB plot was conceived and executed by KGB General Orlov.

Mention should be made that it was General Orlov who personally introduced Ernest Hemingway to the world of guerrilla warfare during the Spanish Civil War and laid the foundation for Hemingway's part fictional novel, *For Whom the Bell Tolls*. It was not until late 1998 that the information concerning Hemingway's relationship with the KGB was cleared by the FBI Pre-Publication Review Board.

One of General Orlov's primary functions during the Spanish Civil War was the establishment of guerrilla warfare training camps in Republican Spain and to command the guerrilla forces deployed against Generalissimo Franco's Nationalist Army. General Orlov is considered the father of modern-day guerrilla warfare.

General Orlov was in Spain during the height of Stalin's great purges when it became apparent to him that he was also about to be liquidated. He broke with the Soviet Government on July 12, 1938 and made his way to the United States where he was granted political asylum. Orlov hid from the KGB and was in constant fear for his life for the following 30 years until the KGB finally tracked him down in Ann Arbor, Michigan in November 1969. Within a week of the contact he fled to another secret location in Cleveland, Ohio where it took the KGB another 2 years to again locate him. He made his final escape from the KGB when he passed away in 1973 under very suspicious circumstances. The author always felt the plight of his hiding and being continually on the run from the KGB for all those years was more abstruse and exciting than the TV series, "The Fugitive."

It was in Cleveland in 1971 when the KGB General and the FBI Agent finally crossed paths. From an antagonistic beginning a warm friendship developed over a period of 2 years. I was at Orlov's bedside during the entire period of his last illness, buried him and subsequently had his personal memoirs and papers sealed in the National Archives for a period of 25 years. I also served as Administrator of the Orlov estate and currently serve as Trustee of the Alexander Orlov Charitable Trust which holds the publishing rights to his personal memoirs as well as published works.

At great personal risk to himself, Orlov's revelations in April of 1953 were published in a 4-part series of articles in Life magazine exposing the atrocities of Soviet Dictator Josef Stalin. This was followed by the publication of his book, *The Secret History of Stalin's Crimes*, the same year which in time was published around the world. For perhaps the first time the world was exposed to the horrors of Stalin's brutal massacre of his own people. During the Cold War Orlov's disclosures were of such magnitude that the Voice of America beamed this information to the people behind the Iron Curtain, making it a most effective tool in combating our enemy at a perilous time in history. The downside of Orlov's quest to publicize the dreadful deeds of Stalin by partially coming in from the cold was that the KGB now could focus their attention in the United States to find the elusive General.

Orlov's achievements on behalf of the Free World did not go unnoticed. The United States Senate cited General Orlov as being one of the most important witnesses ever to testify before the Senate Internal Security Subcommittee investigating subversion in the United States. History will make the final judgment but there is no doubt he is an important historical figure of our time and he left his imprint on history. The U. S. Senate considered General Orlov's contribution to the security of the U.S. of such magnitude that in August 1973, shortly after his death, the Committee of the Judiciary, Ninety-Third Congress, took the extraordinary measure to publish a 150-page Committee Print titled The Legacy of Alexander Orlov, as a final tribute to the General. Indeed, this was a rare tribute to a man who called the United States his home. As in life Orlov remained a mysterious figure even in death, no doubt taking many secrets to his grave. However, in death Orlov managed to have the last laugh on his arch enemy the KGB.

When General Orlov died in 1973 he was cremated. I, with the assistance of a fellow member of the United States intelligence community, had a portion of Orlov's ashes secretly taken to the USSR where they were clandestinely buried in Gorky Park in Moscow in the very shadow of the old Lubyanka Headquarters of the KGB. In life Orlov vowed he would never visit his homeland unless conditions changed in Russia. In 1973 conditions in the USSR had not changed but, nevertheless, Orlov did return to the Soviet Union in a roundabout way after his death. There is little doubt that the KGB would be really riled to know that in spite of its very best efforts to lure its Master Spy back to the Soviet Union, it was its staunchest adversaries who accomplished the feat.

Appendix D: Vouching Letters

LETTER FROM ALEXANDER WEISSBERG

[**Editor's note:** Prosecutor (Procurator) Shpigel's added the following note the file.] The declaration of Citizen Weissberg and documents (nine pages total) were received personally by comrade Shpigel' and he ordered that it be included in the file.]

On May 26, 1936 my former wife Eva Aleksandrovna SHTRIKKER, an Austrian citizen and an artist-consultant at the People's Commissariat for Local Production, was arrested in Moscow.
Because the life of E.A. SHTRIKKER is well known to me, because I have had close relations with her until recently, and because I know her as an honest person who completely supports Soviet power and Communism, I consider it my duty to notify you of the following:
Since my student days I myself have been connected with the workers' movement. I became a member of the Austrian Communist Party on May 1, 1927 and a member of the German Communist Party on December 1, 1929. After I completed my studies, I worked at the Higher Technical Institute in Berlin as a physicist. In 1931, with the sanction of my party organization, I took a job offered to me by the Director of the Ukrainian Technical Institute for Physics. I have worked almost six years as a physicist at the Institute, as a researcher in the area of low temperatures. At the end of 1931, working together with two comrades, citizens of the USSR, I founded the The Journal of Physics of the USSR, the central organ of Soviet physicists, and, until the end of 1934, I served as editor. At the same time, I organized a technical section serving the needs of the chemical and gas industries in our cold laboratory. At the end of 1934, I proposed that the People's Commissariat of Heavy Industry build an experimental station in Kharkov for deep cooling/refrigeration for continuing this research on an industrial scale. The People's Commissariat of Heavy Industry accepted my proposal and I was a Head of Industry, a position I continue to hold.
I met E.A. SHTRIKKER in Berlin among a group of artists and writers with leftist tendencies in which a number of communists were always

present. She completed gymnasium in Budapest, spent a year at the Academy of Arts, and then became an apprentice to a master ceramicist. After receiving the title of journeyman, she worked 18 months at the Kispester Ceramics Factory in Hungary. She then moved to Germany in order to study the technical processes of porcelain production from beginning to end. After nine years of work she gained a great reputation as an artist in the area of designing porcelain for mass production. Her designs for tea and table services have been reproduced and discussed in the specialist literature. She moved in circles of revolutionary artists, belonged to a socialist youth group, and deeply sympathized with the Soviet Union.

Her long-time burning wish was to travel to the USSR and work there in the arena of the creation and diffusion of porcelain production for the needs of the widest population. In March 1931 I arrived in Kharkov. At the end of the year, after I received an apartment from the Institute, my wife followed me to the USSR.

In the Soviet Union she completely devoted herself to the artistic goals placed before her, working tirelessly, never stopping even in the face of greatest limitations and difficulties, overcoming all obstacles, including bureaucratically minded elements and backward colleagues at work, struggling for new forms and an authentically Soviet art in the arena of porcelain. In 1932 she worked at the Ukrainian Glass and Porcelain Trust in Kharkov, who sent her on a business trip to the Lomonosov Porcelain Factory in Leningrad. In the fall of 1934 we separated and E.A. SHTRIKKER accepted a job offer from the Dulevo Porcelain Factory of the People's Commissariat of Local Production.

We have maintained close, friendly relations and are still close to this day.

Knowing very well her life, her character, her thoughts, her ideology and the circle of her interests, I consider it impossible for her to have engaged in hostile activities against the Soviet Union, the country which became her second and true motherland. I am speaking here not only of the "loyalty of a foreign specialist," but of a person who has devoted all of her energy to building socialism.

All comrades who know E.A. SHTRIKKER, among them more than a few occupying responsible, leading posts in the Soviet apparatus and the Comintern, completely share my opinion.

I have written this letter with full knowledge [of its implications of my responsibility], but it is my conviction that since we are speaking of an honest person who has fervently supported the Soviet Union, it is my responsibility to do this.

A.S. Weissberg, September 20, 1936

• • •

TESTIMONIAL

Eva Aleksandrovna Shtriker, with whom I met many times is a person who holds the Soviet world view.

I do not doubt that her entry in the Soviet Union was in order to devote her energies to the building of our country and that this desire defined all her actions.

Academician A. Frumkin , July 18, 1936

• • •

TESTIMONIAL

TO THE NKVD INVESTIGATOR OF THE LENINGRAD REGION
I have been a member of the GCP [German Communist Party] since 1926 and since 1935 I have worked at a scientific director of the Ukrainian Technical Institute for Physics (16 Chaikovskaia Street, Kharkov). Since I arrived in the Soviet Union, I have been registered as a member of the German section of the Comintern.

I know Eva Aleksandrovna SHTRIKKER, her family, and her circle of acquaintances. I can testify that E.A. SHTRIKKER is honest and deeply committed to socialist construction by specialists who devote all their energies and ideas to this project and who have engaged in no hostile activities against the country.

F.O. Houtermanns, September 20, 1936

[Editor's note: Dr. Friedrich Houtermanns (1903-1966), like Weissberg a physicist and an anti-fascist, was arrested on December 1, 1937. Both were handed over to the Gestapo in January, 1940. Houtermans, together with his fellow prisoner Konstantin Shteppa, published his own experiences in NKVD prisons under the pseudonyms F. Beck and W. Godin, RussianPurge..., trans. Eric Mosbacher and David Porter, New York: The Viking Press, 1951.]

• • •

TO THE NKVD INVESTIGATOR OF THE LENINGRAD REGION

Knowing that at the present time the NKVD is investigating the case of E.A. Shtrikker, I consider it necessary to inform you of the following:
I have been acquainted with E.A. Shtrikker for several years since she arrived in the Soviet Union and consider her to be completely Soviet-minded, with an authentic enthusiasm, giving all of her energies to socialist construction. I have no doubt that she is completely loyal to the Soviet Union.

   Academician A.N. Bakn Acad. A Frumkin Member of the Presidium of the Academy of Sciences

• • •

TESTIMONIAL

I met Eva Aleksandrovna SHTRIKER in 1928 in Hamburg where I was working at the Office of the [Soviet] Trade Representative. E.A. Shtriker was employed in a ceramics workshop in Hamburg as a worker at the bench. I found her to be an honest person who sympathized with us. More recently, she has lived in Moscow, and although I have met with her only rarely, in these few meetings I always had the impression that she lived entirely for her work and was completely loyal to our construction and to uplifting our level of life.

   E.L. Seidler Director of the Office of Quality Steels and Hardware of UNIONMETIMPORT Member of the Bolshevik Party since 1931 Supporter of the Communist Party since 1918

• • •

LETTER

I have personally known Eva Aleksandrovna Shtrikker since she arrived in the USSR in 1932. I have met with her in Leningrad, Moscow, and Kharkov. She always impressed me as being full of enthusiasm for working for the betterment of our country and devoting all of her energies and abilities to this. All of her work, it seems to me, completely represents this.

Professor Y.I. Frenkel Corresponding Member of the USSR Academy of Sciences Leningrad, Industrial Institute, apt. 3 September 1936

• • •

USSR Academy of Sciences, Institute of Biochemistry
Inst. Address: 75 Great Kaluga St., Moscow 71 Tel. – B-5-32-04 —
Director's Office Director—Academician A.N. BAKH B-5-32-07—General number
June 17, 1936

TESTIMONIAL[S]

I have been acquainted with Eva Aleksandrovna SHTRIKER for several years and I know her as a worker completely sympathetic to the Soviet cause and an authentic enthusiasm for devoting all of her energies and her specialty to socialist construction.
ACADEMICIAN: A. Bakh /A.N. Bakh/
[Handwritten addition by Ioffe at bottom of Bakh's letter.]
Having known Eva Aleksandrovna Shtriker for several years since her arrival in the USSR, I am in complete agreement with the testimonial of Academician A.N. Bakh.
Academician A. Ioffe   (A.F. Ioffe

Appendix E: Weimar Berlin

by Eva Zeisel

Berlin, at that time, was fat, obsessed with modernity, and a fad of sexual permissiveness. The words of a refrain sung, while frantically dancing the shimmy, by the chorus of the cabaret The Blue Angel: "Time is money, Sein Sie Mein" [be mine] might be as good as any to describe Berlin's pace and spirit.

But Berlin was also buzzing with contradictions. The repulsive characters of George Grosz (the ugly rich); the haggard mothers of Kate Kollwitz; the lonely men lost in the "big city" of Mazzareel—all these groups of people lived in different parts of town, far from the lights of the chic town center. And so did the drab class of déclassé office holders and pensioners, who lived their dreary lives within their families, hiding their poverty (the result of incredible inflation a few years back) under a thin skin of respectability, described by the writer Anna Seghers.

However, there also lived then in Berlin hundreds of gifted young people as concerned and sympathetic as Grosz, Kollwitz, Masereel, and Seghers. The town abounded in talented people with typical German sentimentality and pseudo cynicism. The Threepenny Opera expressed the brassy lifestyle of the town, and the concern for the breakdown of long-standing moral values, the desperation of a disoriented generation of do-gooders by singing "*Erst kommt das Fressen und Dann kommt die Moral*!" (first you gobble food, then comes morality).

The German Expressionists painted their comments with spatula and broad brushstrokes on their painfully ugly canvasses. At the same time other artists performed feats of great beauty with the highest skills and refinement, like the concerts of Casals, or Marie Wigman's disciplined movements or Breuer's esoteric, modern apartments for rich, young sophisticated couples where everything floated in shadowless space, or the pure, white villas and the luxurious Barcelona chair. All of these designs were rooted in a new theory, the Puritan, social-minded program called the *Neue Sachlichkeit*, originally aimed at bringing healthy housing and standardized useful things to the poor. Meanwhile, the *Künstlerfeste*, Artists' Feasts, looked like huge orgies, with elaborate costumes covering their frustrations, permitting anonymous, make believe, hedonistic carpe diem illusions, at least for that one night.

From the influx of a large number of Russian émigrés grew a fad for all things Russian: Russian entertainers in restaurants and nightclubs, the monumental chorus of the Don Cossacks, popular songs and lullabies, all brought strange sounds, costumes and colors and a fresh, bright mood of Russian folk ways into the mishmash of Berlin's culture and counterculture. These were a contrast to the angry Expressionists and the (alleged) cynicism of the Threepenny Opera. Soviet Russia also sent lovely children's books and the exquisitely chiseled performances of its theaters, as well as the novel imagery of Kandinsky and Tatlin. All this seemed to originate in a vigorous, healthy source in an unknown, far away country striving towards a Utopia where justice was going to reign.

Such influences, rather than the propagandistic descriptions of Soviet Russia in the Communist newspaper *Rote Fahne*, had a much greater impact on many young intellectuals.

At that time, everyone was explicitly committed to one or another political opinion and usually belonged to one of the parties. The political atmosphere was becoming alarming, although among us the reality of a Nazi takeover still appeared far away. One of our acquaintances, a wealthy student, bought large quantities of canned goods against the prospect of a Communist takeover, but this was far-fetched.

During these excited times, Berlin attracted intellectuals from many countries, becoming for a while, the cultural center of the West, and the *Romanisches Café* was its Forum Romanum. Since my atelier was but a few houses from it, Koestler and other friends often met there. Most of the friends Arthur met at my studio on Tauentsienstrasse 8, believed that they were personally in charge of solving the world's social and political problems. They would have been, I believe, surprised, possibly even offended, if told that no one had put this burden on their shoulders or that they might not be competent to bear it. Each believed that he was individually responsible for the world and each propounded his ideology, ideas or system. Leo Szilard, for instance, proposed a Wellsian idea that the best minds in the world should be in charge of the world's affairs. Alex Weissberg who with equal gusto liked to declaim Rilke and Shakespeare for hours, indulged in sharing his thorough knowledge of the Third International Congresses, and squabbles in the history in the programs of the Communist Party, with whoever was willing to listen. It was from him that Arthur learned its tenets. Later he shared with Alex his deep disappointment with the Communist Party. They had become close friends in Berlin in 1931. It was an extraordinary conglomeration of people who came together there. Even many years later, some of them continued to offer advice about how to run the world to those who were willing to hear them, such as Szilard, who composed the Einstein letter to Roosevelt, which led to the development of the atom bomb, and who later tried to prevent the dropping of the bomb on a populated area, and finally went to advise Khrushchev how to keep the peace. Khrushchev eventually returned the visit, coming to Szilard's New York City hospital room, presenting him with a case of Russian mineral water. Or Victor (Weisskopf) who offered the benefits of his learning to Pope John Paul and who was sent as the Pope's emissary to President Reagan, to explain to him how to prevent the world from being destroyed.

That year (1931) among my friends, Arthur felt least responsible for the affairs of the world, having somehow circumnavigated the influence of the then very lively Social Democratic youth movement, which had been nourished by the successful, Socialist Viennese administration and it's ideologues. He had spent his high school years outside Vienna and, during his university years he was involved with Zionism, which really was concerned only with part of humanity, unlike the rest of my friends who wanted to save it all.

This is part of a letter I wrote to Hans [Zeisel] when I was living in Berlin:

> Abends war ich mit dem Koestler im Romanischen. Und stellte fest dass er von uns allen der traurigste ist. Es scheint hier diese Hoffnungslosigkeit sehr allgemein und echt zu sein. Man kann wohl jetzt doch nur nach Russland fahren, sonst ist man scheinbar zu dieser fatalen Stimmung verpflichtet.

[I spent the evening with Koestler in the *Romanisches Café* and realized that, of all of us, he is the saddest. It seems that the feeling of hopelessness here is widespread and genuine. All that is left is to go to Russia; otherwise one becomes part of this fatalistic atmosphere.]

Further Reading

HISTORY

Alliluyeva, Svetlana. *Twenty* Letters To A Friend. (London: Hutchison, 1967).

Beck, F. and Godin, W. (pseudonyms for cellmates physicist Friedrich Houtermanns, and historian Konstantin Shteppa) Russian Purge and the Extraction of Confession. trans. Eric Mosbacher and David Porter (New York: The Viking Press, 1951).

Farago, Ladislas. *The Game of the Foxes*. (London: Hodder & Stoughton, 1972).

Gazur, Edward P. *Secret Assignment: The FBI's KGB General*. (London: St. Erman's Press and Little, Brown & Company, 2001. New York: Carroll and Graf Publishers, 2002).

Kettering, Karen. *Eva Zeisel: The Playful Search for Beauty*. (Knoxville, TN: Knoxville Museum of Art, 2004).

Koestler, Arthur. *Darkness At Noon*. (New York: The New American Library, 1941, 1961).

Orlov, Alexander. *The Secret History of Stalin's Crimes*. (New York: Random House, 1953). *Tainaia istoriia stalinskikh prestuplenii* (Sankt-Petersburg: Vsemirnoe slovo, 1991).

Szapor, Judith. *The Hungarian Pocahontas*: *The Life and Times of Laura Polanyi Stricker, 1882-1959*. (Berkeley, CA: University Presses of California, Columbia and Princeton, 2005).

Weissberg, Alexander, Trans. Edward Fitzgerald. *The Accused*. (New York: Simon and Schuster, 1951).

Weisskopf, Victor. *The Joy of Insight*. (New York: HarperCollins Publishers, 1991). pp. 56-58.

BOOKS BY AND ABOUT EVA ZEISEL (WEB)

Eidelberg, Martin. *Eva Zeisel: Designer for Industry*. (Chicago, IL: University of Chicago Press (dist.), 1984). Out-of-print.

Kirkham, P., Moore, P., Wolfframm, P. *Eva Zeisel: Life, Design, and Beauty*. (San Francisco, CA: Chronicle Books, in preparation).

Young, Lucie. *Eva Zeisel: The Playful Search for Beauty*. (San Francisco, CA: Chronicle Books, 2003).

Zeisel, Eva. *Eva Zeisel: On Design*. (New York: Overlook, 2004, 2011, paperback).

FILM AND VIDEO

Throwing Curves. A documentary film about Eva Zeisel by Jyll Johnstone, available through Canobie Films.

Authors / Compilers

EVA ZEISEL (WEB)

Eva Zeisel (1906-2011) is considered one of the major designers of the 20th and early 21st centuries. Although known primarily for her ceramics, she has designed furniture, rugs, wood, glass and metalware for factories around the world. Her designs are in collections of many major museums.

Born in Budapest, she emigrated to the U.S. in 1938, where she went on to design tableware for mass production. From 1940-1952 she taught "Ceramics For Industry" at the Pratt Institute. In 1946 her porcelain "Museum Shape" was shown in a one-woman show at the Museum of Modern Art. Her 1950's Hallcraft set became the best-selling set in the country." Eva's more recent designs are now on the market. Her older designs are widely collected.

She is the author of Eva Zeisel On Design (Overlook Press, 2004), which is based on her many lectures. For more information contact Eva Zeisel Forum, .

JEAN RICHARDS (WEB)

Jean Richards, Eva's daughter, is an actress and writer. She has appeared on, off and off-off Broadway in plays and musicals, as well as recording many voice-overs, including for over 200 children's books. She is the author of several children's books, among them God's Gift (Bantam, Doubleday Dell), a Children's Book Of The Month Club Main Selection, and A Fruit Is A Suitcase For Seeds (Lerner Publishers). She also adapted the Magic SchoolBus series for audio production.

DR. KAREN KETTERING

Dr. Karen Kettering is the former Vice President in Sotheby's Russian Department and Specialist in Russian Works of Art, Fabergé, and Icons. From 1998 to 2007, she served as a Curator of Russian and Eastern European Art at Washington D.C.'s Hillwood Museum & Gardens, where she organized the exhibition The Myths of St. Petersburg and Eva Zeisel:

The Playful Search for Beauty, a retrospective of Zeisel's career including her stints working in the Soviet Union and the Russian Federation. Her publications cover many aspects of Russian decorative arts, including a recent book on the Imperial Palaces at Bialowieza and Spala, multiple articles on Russian and Soviet porcelain, the workshop of Russian silversmith Maria Semyonova, a history of Russian glass, the architecture and interiors of the Moscow Metro, contemporary icon painters in Yaroslavl, and the sale of Russian decorative arts in nineteenth-century America.

EDWARD P. GAZUR

The late Edward P. Gazur was a career FBI Special Agent. His primary focus was Eastern European espionage and counterespionage. In the 1970s, Gazur was assigned to protect and debrief the highest ranking officer to defect from the KGB [NKVD], General Alexander Orlov. He also worked on the investigation of the assassination of President John F. Kennedy. Gazur was born in Cleveland, Ohio, and lived in Kentucky with his wife, Ruth, a former employee of the FBI.

BRENT C. BROLIN (WEB)

Brent C. Brolin practiced architecture in the dim past, then wrote 7 books trying to explain to himself why he had been taught what he had been taught in architecture school (Yale '68). One or another of these books has been translated into Serbo Croatian, German, Greek, Chinese or Spanish. His photographs illustrate his books, as well as culture critic Howard Kissel's New York Theatre Walks (Applause Books, 2007), an entertaining book about theatre-related, New York neighborhoods, and Eva Zeisel: Life, Design, and Beauty (Chronicle Books, 2013). Eva Zeisel: A Soviet Prison Memoir was his first eBook; this is the first iBook edition.

www.ingramcontent.com/pod-product-compliance
Lightning Source LLC
Chambersburg PA
CBHW071419040426
42331CB00050B/2601